Mindfulness
for Stress
Management

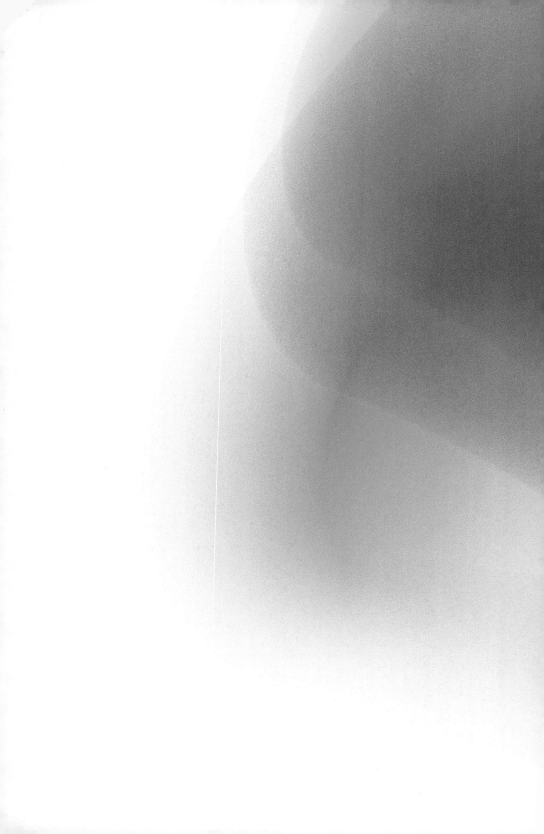

Mindfulness for Stress Management

50 Ways to Improve Your Mood and Cultivate Calmness

Dr. Robert Schachter

ALTHEA
PRESS

Interior and Cover Designer: Antonio Valverde

Art Producer: Sara Feinstein

Editor: Lia Ottaviano

Production Editor: Andrew Yackira

ISBN: Print 978-1-64152-569-5 | eBook 978-1-64152-570-1

*To Wendi, Ilana,
and Chloe,
the women who
inspire me*

Contents

Introduction

Stress is a part of normal, everyday life. If you are reading this book, stress must be interfering with a large part of your life, and if that is true, you may be suffering more than you need to. There is no end to the possibilities that cause stress. For example, you might need to take each of your three children to three different soccer games, or perhaps you have work assignments that are due when you don't have enough time to do them, or maybe you are caring for an ill or elderly parent.

The good news is that even though these situations are demanding, they do not have to be stressful. With the powerful methods you will learn in this book, you can reduce stress and its effects on you.

I became fascinated with treating stress over 10 years ago when my mother had dangerously high blood pressure. She had tried several medicines, but her blood pressure remained high. Her life was extremely stressful. She ran a large company and was constantly encountering and solving problems. I knew that stress was causing her blood pressure problem, and I was concerned about her.

One day at Mount Sinai, where I am on the faculty at Icahn School of Medicine, I started researching all the possible ways to treat stress. It was then that I discovered mindfulness. I found many evidence-based studies that showed mindfulness could have a dramatic effect on reducing stress and lowering blood pressure. I read as much about it as I could. I participated in workshops and learned the art of using mindfulness.

I taught my mother how to practice mindfulness, and her blood pressure fell to normal. I started incorporating these simple yet very effective methods into my work by teaching them to my patients. I found stress to be a pervasive problem for so many people that I founded the Stress Centers of New York. I have seen dramatic results with my patients, and in this book I will teach you the same techniques so you can conquer your own stress.

Chapter 1

Getting Started

When you are in a stressful situation, you evaluate it. When your mind assesses it as problematic, you start to feel stress. Your body then responds automatically—something over which you do not have control. Mindfulness is a practice that teaches you how to stay completely in the present moment. It creates distance from your upsetting thoughts and gives you a way to be in control of both your mind and your body. One advantage to using this approach is that you can do it anytime, anywhere.

In this book you will learn the methods of mindfulness as well as understand the core characteristics and principles of this powerful approach. I will help you understand the body and brain's responses to stress. You also will become familiar with the basics of mindfulness and how this approach combats stress and neutralizes its effects on both your mind and your body.

As simple as mindfulness is to learn, this will be a new experience for you, and it will take some practice. It may be a few weeks or perhaps longer before you find yourself applying it automatically. So, have patience with yourself. Once mindfulness becomes a regular habit, it will change your life.

With this book, I invite you to learn the simple yet very powerful tools to reduce stress and remove its unhealthy effects from your life. It can change how you feel in ways you never imagined.

What Is Mindfulness?

Mindfulness means being aware of your thoughts without the distractions that normally create tension and stress. Mindfulness is the art of staying in the present moment, with your awareness focused on whatever your senses are experiencing. Your mind becomes a neutral, nonjudgmental observer of everything that passes in front of it. It is being open in a way you are not yet accustomed to and allows you to avoid an unhealthy amount of stress.

Each component of mindfulness is designed to allow you to be open. One component is a concept called beginner's mind. If you were to see things as though your mind were a blank slate, with no preconceptions, and you were open to each experience as though you had never experienced it before, you would have a beginner's mind.

Another component is the art of having patience, or being able to slow the increasingly fast pace of your life.

Mindfulness asks you to be nonjudgmental of everything. Judging things and people is one of the ways you may define yourself, and doing so can take up enormous space in your mind. Suspending judgment is another tool for remaining present in the moment.

Trust in yourself is also an important part of a mindfulness practice. It means letting go and simply believing in your own intuition.

Non-striving is another fundamental part of mindfulness. It means allowing yourself to be in the present moment rather than trying to make something different happen. It is being where you are instead of running toward a goal.

Accepting how things are, rather than thinking about how to change them, is a basic aspect of being in the present moment. Letting go of disappointment from unmet expectations is critical in accepting the present moment. It also is particularly freeing.

Letting go, or freeing your mind from everything it holds on to, is the final element. You may cling to your identity as you know it. You may clutch your beliefs. You may hold on to your grudges and old angers. Letting go is one more way to free yourself of the ways you can remain stuck in the past.

As you learn these different aspects of mindfulness, you will be able to stop the stress caused by a constant stream of negative thinking. Your worries, your concerns, your problems all conspire to take away your peace of mind. The practice of mindfulness can give it back to you, or it can give it to you for the first time.

Your Body on Stress

No matter the source of stress, your body's reaction is always the same. In stressful situations, a complex hormonal physiological response occurs as your body prepares you to fend off an attack, activating all the abilities you need to survive.

As your body goes on high alert, adrenaline surges through you. Your breathing becomes more rapid to bring more oxygen into your lungs, and your blood pressure increases. Your pancreas pours sugar into your system to give you more energy. Your muscles tense, ready to spring into action.

During the first stages of stress, you can perform better. You may think more clearly, have more energy, and be more actively engaged. After a stressful situation passes, your body returns to normal. If the stress continues, however, as it often does in today's fast-paced and complicated world, your body stays on high alert, which depletes your resources. Chronic stress can lower your immune system and cause muscle tension and other problems. You may experience memory impairment, depression, skin conditions such as eczema, difficulty sleeping, obesity, heart disease, digestive problems, irritable bowel syndrome, exacerbation of Crohn's disease, insomnia, type 2 diabetes, chronic muscle tightness, and much more. Just thinking about all the possible stress-related health problems can cause a great deal of stress.

Ultimately, chronic stress causes burnout. Burnout occurs when chronic stress reaches a critical stage. It starts with feeling disconnected at work and in relationships. You become more irritable, withdrawn, and depressed. Some people engage in destructive behavior at this stage, perhaps drinking alcohol excessively or abusing drugs. They may miss work or partake of other harmful behaviors.

Mindfulness has been proven to relieve many of the effects of stress on the body. Take a moment here to be proud of yourself for seeking relief from stress and its unhealthy effects. You have taken an important step toward better health and a better life—for yourself and others around you. The exercises you will learn in this book will help you achieve the stress relief you seek. It is never too late to learn mindfulness or resume a practice you may have once started but discontinued. You will need to continue using these techniques until they become habit. Mindfulness takes discipline, but the benefits will astound you.

How Mindfulness Can Help

Any approach to emotional or behavioral modification needs to be based on evidence. Mindfulness has been researched extensively, and the results have been dramatic.

In a study published in the *Journal of Behavioral Health* in 2013, a mindfulness program was shown to significantly reduce the stress levels of oncology nurses. All the nurses in this study were surveyed at three points: the starting point, eight weeks after starting the program, and four months after starting the program. The nurses were asked about overall health, stress levels, burnout, self-compassion, serenity, and empathy.

The results showed measurable improvements in the overall health and wellness of the nurses at each point of the study. In addition, the nurses who continued their mindfulness practice after four months showed even better outcomes than the nurses who did not continue the program.

Another study published in 2011 in *Fertility and Sterility* showed impressive results for women about to undergo in vitro fertilization (IVF) who used mindfulness techniques. In this study, 143 women aged 40 years or younger were about to begin their first IVF treatment. The women were randomly grouped into either a 10-session mind/body program or a control group. All the women were followed for two IVF cycles. The pregnancy rates for women in the mind/body program was 52 percent, compared to 20 percent for the control group.

Another clinical trial published in *Stress and Health* in 2019 compared stress-related symptoms in women aged 18 to 50 years who participated in an eight-week mindfulness-based program against symptoms of women who did not. The group in the mindfulness-based program demonstrated significantly reduced stress-related symptoms while the other group showed no significant change.

Making the Most of This Book

Learning how to use mindfulness to significantly reduce stress might be one of the most important things you ever do for yourself. This book is designed as an easy guide to learning the different exercises that will allow you to separate yourself from your stressful thoughts and emotions. Do bear in mind that you will be learning a new skill, and that can take time and effort, so be committed and have patience.

SIMPLE, STEP-BY-STEP EXERCISES

Each chapter presents exercises that address a different aspect of combating stress. Each exercise includes a brief description; the time it will take to complete it; and simple, step-by-step instructions. Some exercises will teach you how to heal your body from the ravages of stress. Others will help you conquer stressful thoughts. Different exercises work differently for different people, so you need to try them all to find the most effective ones for you.

You have the desire to reduce stress in your life. Now you have the power to achieve this by changing the way your mind perceives and deals with stressful situations. So far, you have read about the power of mindfulness and how it can help stop the harmful ways stress affects you. Now, you will learn the methods of mindfulness and how to apply them in everyday situations.

There are two parts to learning any new skill. The first part is learning how to use the skill. The other, more important part is how to stop using the pattern that the skill is replacing. Remember that you may be replacing patterns you have used for many years. If you are unsure about devoting time and energy to learn how to incorporate mindfulness into your life, just think of all the time and energy you have devoted to dealing with stress. Think of all the demands stress makes on your body and your life.

You may not immediately see the results of your Mindfulness practice. Some have compared learning the techniques to exercising a muscle; the more you practice, the more automatic it becomes. It is important to give yourself a time frame of several weeks to truly understand the approach and see results.

Chapter
2

Healing the Stressful Body

Stress can take a tremendous toll on your body and your life. A research project at Carnegie Mellon University found that chronic psychological stress is associated with the loss of the body's ability to regulate the inflammatory response. The research shows that this can promote the development and progression of disease. This was the first study to definitively show that men who experience persistently moderate or high levels of stressful life events over a number of years have a 50 percent higher rate of earlier mortality.

Another study definitively showed that stress impedes healing. This study used different wound-healing models. There was a significant difference in a wound-healing experiment between those subjected to stress and those who were not.

Mindfulness has been proven to relieve many of the effects of stress on the body, which is why it is important for you to learn and then continue to use these exercises until they become habit. The benefits will more than repay your determination.

1

Just Breathe

Time

5 Minutes

Best for

Preventing chronic stress

One of the major tools available to you for a mindful state is your breath. Remember that the objective of a mindfulness practice is to turn off your mind and allow yourself to be still. Focusing only on your breath allows that to happen. When you focus on your physical act of breathing, it is more difficult to go into your thoughts. There are several different ways to explore your breath as a pathway to being in the present moment.

1. Find a quiet place where you can comfortably sit or lie down.

2. Start by breathing normally. Notice how it feels. Feel the warmth as air enters your nostrils and throat. Notice where you feel your breath in your body—your chest or your abdomen.

3. Follow the breath as it enters your lungs and then feel the sensations as you follow it from your lungs out through your nose or mouth. Let all your attention focus on the breath. Notice as one breath ends and the next begins.

4. Sense the breath as a quality of motion. Notice how it moves in the different parts of your body as you breathe in a steady rhythm.

5. Now inhale through your mouth while counting to 4: 1, 2, 3, 4. Then count backward on the exhale: 4, 3, 2, 1. Try to breathe very slowly. The goal is to focus on the sensations that you feel at each point. Do this for 5 minutes.

6. After several days, increase the length of time you inhale, exhale, and hold the breath. Start by holding the breath as you count to 5. Slowly exhale as you count to 5. Do this for 5 minutes. After several days, increase gradually to a total of 10 minutes. Practice this exercise twice each day.

HARNESSING YOUR BREATH

If you breathe more deeply and let the area around your stomach expand, you are pulling the air in and pushing it out with your diaphragm. When you catch your mind wandering, gently bring your focus back to your breath. Breathe in through your nose slowly and feel the sensation of the air as it travels to your lungs. To bring in as much oxygen as possible, be aware of the point where you need to breathe more deeply. Place one hand on your stomach and the other on your chest. As you take a breath in, you should feel the hand on your stomach rise beyond the other one, and when you breathe out, it should be lower. Doing this guarantees that you are getting the full benefit of the breath.

2

Calm Eating

Time

10 Minutes

Best for

Conscious consumption

You may find that you don't eat in a mindful way, hurrying through meals without savoring the flavors and textures of the food. In this exercise, you will use all your senses to experience food.

1. Get an orange or another juicy fruit that you like.

2. Pick up the orange. Look at it. Look at its roundness. See the texture and all the tiny creases in the skin. Notice the variations in color, as if you were going to paint it from memory.

3. Feel the texture of the skin. What does it feel like to run your fingers over it? Concentrate on the sensations on your fingertips. Staying focused, tear a piece of the skin from the top of the orange. Feel the tension on your fingernails and the change in pressure as the skin gives way. Experience the difference between the toughness of the skin and the softness of the flesh under it.

4. Bring the orange to your nose. Can you smell anything? Tear a larger strip of skin. Now smell the open orange. Let the layers of fragrance linger in your nose. Note the variations in fragrance as minutes go by.

5. Let all thoughts drift away. If you find yourself thinking of something, redirect your focus to the orange. Now taste the juice. What sensations take the stage? Let the layers of flavor wander over your tongue. Is it sweet? Is it bitter? Now take a small bite of the orange. Chew it until there is no pulp left.

6. Squeeze the orange, allowing the juice to fall into a glass. Feel the pressure on the palm of your hand. Watch the juice and its motion. Listen for the sounds. Watch the flow of the juice. Now drink the juice. Again, pay attention with all five senses, one at a time. When you follow these steps, you are eating in the moment.

3

Come to Your Senses

Time

5 Minutes

Best for

Staying present

With this exercise, you will learn how to use all your senses to still your mind. Paying attention to all your senses allows you to be present in the moment. This exercise will enable you to lower your stress by getting out of your head and just being with yourself and your experience. You can practice this every day for about five minutes. Because it will relax you, you may take more time, and that is fine.

1. Pick the day and time when you will do this sensory experiment and choose where you want to do it. It can be where you live or in another location, perhaps in a city or in the country or at a beach.

2. Find a comfortable place to sit. Close your eyes and open yourself up to any sensation through any one of your senses. Listen to any sounds. Are they high sounds, scratchy sounds, chirpy sounds? Let your mind just focus on listening. Listen to the sounds change as one comes into focus and as another takes over. Pay attention to any sounds in the background. Is there a plane flying overhead, or are there horns honking? Is it quiet?

3. Move your awareness to any scents. What do you smell? Try to notice each scent as though you have never smelled it before. If you are in the city, do you smell car exhaust? If you are in the country, do you smell trees or grass? You may have to make a conscious effort because you may not usually pay attention to smell unless it is overpowering and bad.

4. Open your eyes. Look around with intention. Notice the shapes, the colors. Take in the sight of something as though it is the first time you have ever seen it.

5. Now touch an object or surface. Notice the texture. Is it smooth? Bumpy?

6. As you move through this exercise, notice any thoughts that float in. As with the other exercises, observe your thoughts and let them go. Come back to your senses.

4

A Walk in the Park

Time

5 Minutes

Best for

Mindfulness while walking

The art of reducing stress is to stay as mindful as you can throughout the day. Doing this when you walk is a wonderful way to continue to stay relaxed and to reduce stress. Normally, when you are walking, you are just thinking of getting to where you are going, and your mind is filled with thoughts of the past or future. The goal of this exercise is to keep you in the present and allow your mind to be open to the sensory experiences of walking. There are a lot of moving parts when you walk. You probably never focus on the feeling of your feet touching the ground or the brush of your pants or skirt on your legs. Try this exercise with different types of walking, such as rushing to be somewhere, or when you are angry, or when you are filled with joy. This exercise helps you clear your mind, and you can practice it several times a day or whenever you go for a walk.

1. Start by just standing still. Notice the weight on your feet. Notice your balance. Do you make slight adjustments to stay balanced? Feel the weight of your body on your legs, knees, and ankles.

2. Start walking slowly. Feel the weight on your foot. Notice how your foot touches the ground and stays in contact until you lift it up. Can you notice any other sensations, like the way your feet feel in your shoes? Are they very comfortable, or do they pinch your toes?

3. Notice what your ankle feels like when the ball of your foot touches the ground. How do your thighs or calves feel as you lift your feet and put them down?

4. Pay attention to your knees. What do you feel? Do they ache or feel strong? Do you feel how they help propel your legs?

5. Explore any other physical sensations from your hips and the rest of your body. Notice any thoughts or emotions that arise.

5

A Touching Moment

Time

5 Minutes

Best for

Building sensory awareness through touch

As you continue to explore your senses in the present moment, this exercise will focus on touch. Tactile sensations are the most primitive of all senses. It is the first sense an infant experiences when held by his mother. The sense of touch often dominates over all other senses. This exercise will help you achieve mindfulness through touch. Throughout the exercise, when you find your mind wandering or thinking, note it and let it go.

1. Choose a place to do these explorations. Outdoors might provide more variety, but you can also do them indoors. Stay as focused as you can on the journey you are taking now.

2. Start by standing. Feel your feet connecting you with the ground. Feel the pressure on your toes, on the balls of your feet, on your heels. Concentrate on the sensation. Feel the weight of your clothes, your chest pressing against your shirt as you breathe in. Now, feel the weight of your shoulders as you stand straight. Feel the air entering your lungs, then leaving. Feel any sensation on your face.

3. Begin to walk, and as you walk, touch your legs with your hands. What is the texture of your clothing? Rough? Smooth? Rippled?

4. Find a place to sit. Feel the weight of your body settling onto that place. As you sit, do you feel something hard? Soft? If you are on a chair, what does your back feel as it leans against the chair? If you are sitting on a bed, how does it feel as you sink into the mattress surface?

5. Wrap your arms around yourself. What do your hands feel? Are you wearing a shirt? Is it soft or is it starchier? How do your hands feel as they clasp your arms? What do your arms feel as they are gripped by your hands? Do they feel warm? Are they comforting?

6. Now touch your face. Note the texture. Is it soft? Stubbly?

7. If you are inside, go to the refrigerator. Take out anything cold and hold it. Feel the cold on your hands. Take a towel. Feel the texture. Soak the towel with warm water. Feel the warmth of the water and the softer texture of the towel.

6

Body Scan

Time

5 to 7 Minutes

Best for

Calming your body

One of the key mechanisms for clearing your mind of stress is to focus on your body, because when you are focusing on your body, it is very difficult to focus on your thoughts. This exercise targets the tension you hold in your muscles and allows you to release it.

1. Start by lying or sitting in a comfortable position.

2. Take a slow, deep breath in through your nose. Feel your breath go deeper and let your stomach expand as you breathe in. Slowly let your breath out through your mouth. Do this three times.

3. Notice any physical sensations such as warmth, tingling, or chills. Pay attention to each sensation separately as you notice it. If you feel tension, send it a message to let go. Focus on your hands. Feel the sensations in your fingertips, then your fingers, then your knuckles.

4. Take a deep breath. Feel your stomach expand as you breathe. Let your breath out slowly. Focus your attention on your wrists. Release any tension you feel. Now concentrate on your forearms. Let the tension go.

5. Pay attention to your elbows, the back of your upper arms, and the front of your upper arms. Concentrate now on your biceps and then your shoulders. Continue to take slow, deep breaths.

6. Center your attention on your neck. What sensations do you experience: warmth, tension, tingling? Move up your neck to the base of your skull. Concentrate now on your scalp. Come back down your neck to your shoulders. Slowly move to your upper back, then your lower back.

7. Take a moment. If there is stress there, let it go.

8. Now go to your chest. Take a breath and let tension go. Now, slowly, focus on your abdomen and your core. Bring attention to your hips. Release any tension. Then concentrate on your upper thighs and now your knees and then slowly move to your calves. See if there is tension in your shins or your ankles. Focus on the soles of your feet, the top of your feet, and your toes. Let all your tension drift away.

7

Love Begins
with Yourself

Time

10 Minutes

Best for

Building a strong relationship with yourself

Loving-kindness meditation is the concept of maintaining a mental state of unselfish and unconditional kindness to all beings. To start with loving-kindness, you must begin with yourself. At first, you may feel as though you are going through the motions of feeling self-love. After a short while, though, you will find that the loving thoughts you have been giving yourself start becoming part of your unconscious mind, and then they become part of you.

1. Start by sitting comfortably in a quiet place. Take slow, deep breaths, feeling your stomach expand as you breathe

2. Picture an image of yourself at any time you felt your own self-worth. If you can't remember, think of a time when you were loved by another. Try to be open to it and let the warmth of that feeling spread through your body.

3. Now picture someone who loves or has loved you very much standing on your left side. It could be a relative, a partner, or a child. Picture another person who loves you on your right side.

4. Imagine yourself surrounded by all the people who care about you. Feel their love and say:

   May I be filled with loving-kindness

   May I accept myself just as I am

   May I be safe and healthy

   May I be happy

5. Now picture the people around you. Send love out to them. Say:

   May you be filled with loving-kindness

   May you accept yourself just as you are

   May you be safe and healthy

   May you be happy

6. Picture a person you do not have a connection to, perhaps a stranger. Repeat the words. Now picture someone you do not like. Repeat the words. If this is difficult, come back to the image of yourself and repeat the words.

8

Tense
and Release

Time

5 to 7 Minutes

Best for

Total
relaxation

This exercise is a wonderful way to create a relaxation response to counter the stress response. It takes time to retrain your body's response to tension and stress. When you practice every day, your body develops a memory of being relaxed that will become automatic.

1. Find a quiet place. You can do this exercise either lying down or sitting in a chair.

2. Take a deep breath in through the nose, letting your stomach expand to let your lungs expand fully. Exhale slowly through the mouth. Start with your hands. Make tight fists. Squeeze them for a count of 10, or until it burns a little bit, and release them.

3. Flex your forearms by extending your arms with your hands tilted back toward your head. Hold until you feel a slight burning sensation. Now relax your arms.

4. Flex your biceps. Hold them as if you are a body builder. Hold them for a count of 10. And then release. Lift your shoulders up toward your ears. Hold for a count of 10. Now release.

5. Now, tense the muscles in your face. Make the funniest face that you can and hold it until it burns. Relax your face. Feel the difference between when you are tensed and when you are relaxed.

6. Take another deep breath. Flex your core. Press your arms against your sides and push in while you do a partial sit-up. Feel the muscles tighten in your abdomen. Hold it until it burns slightly. Now release.

7. Take another breath. Flex your buttocks, hold, then release. Extending one leg at a time, flex your thigh, your quadriceps muscle. Hold until you feel tension, then release. Be careful not to get a cramp. Repeat with the other leg. Take another deep breath.

8. Now flex your calf muscles. Point your toes back toward your head. You can do both at the same time. Hold and then release. Finally flex your toes. Hold for a count of 10, then release. Take another breath. Again, note the difference between when you are tensed and when you are relaxed.

9

Mindful Indulgences

Time

15 Minutes

Best for

Relaxing activities

This exercise guides you to stay in the present moment with your body during a relaxing, indulgent activity—in this case, taking a warm bath. Make a list of things you find completely pleasurable. If a relaxing bath is not on your list, use this exercise to guide your own pleasurable activities. Be sure to pay attention to your body and all your senses during the activity. Be completely self-indulgent.

1. Choose a time when you can disconnect from all other distractions. To do this exercise properly, you must be totally self-indulgent. You can't hold back.

2. Start running a bath by choosing the perfect temperature for the water.

3. Turn the lights down. If you have some candles, bring them in and light them.

4. As the water fills the tub, let it flow over your hand. Focus on the sensation of the warmth and notice the water pressure. Is it strong? What does it sound like?

5. Your thoughts of the day may be racing around your head with the plans you need to make for tomorrow. When you catch yourself thinking or planning, just notice it and direct your attention back to the sensations.

6. Would you care for a cool drink in your bath or a warm cup of tea? If you choose tea, pay attention to the steps involved in preparing it. Notice the sound of the teakettle as you open it. Hear the sound of the water coming from the faucet to fill it. Notice the weight of the kettle and how it feels when you place it on the stove or connect it to the wall socket. Smell the tea before you brew it. Stay with the sense of it.

7. If you prefer a cold drink, feel the temperature of the glass on your hand. Listen as you pour the liquid into the glass.

8. When you take a sip, feel the sensation on your lips and in your throat.

9. For any other treat you may like, go through the same process. See, listen, smell, feel, and then taste. At each moment, stay focused on the sensory input. By staying present in the moment, you will find yourself enjoying your favorite activities even more.

10

This Will Put You to Sleep

Time

5 to 10 Minutes

Best for

Getting to sleep

Do you ever have trouble falling asleep? If not, you are lucky. A National Sleep Foundation poll found that 63 percent of women and 54 percent of men experienced insomnia at least a few nights per week. If insomnia is ever a problem, this brief body scan can really help. The steps in this exercise will enhance your mindfulness practice, and it can also help send you to sleep.

1. As you lie in bed, close your eyes. Inhale, using slow, deep breaths. Let your stomach expand as you breathe in. Exhale slowly. Do this five times, very slowly. Your mind will probably wander as you do this. If so, note it and bring your focus back to your breathing. You may need to do this several times. Just breathe.

2. Focus on your body, starting with your toes. If you feel any tension, let it go. Move your focus slowly to your ankles and feet. Same there; if you feel any tension, give it a signal to let it go. Make sure you don't rush through this, as it is important to take time.

3. As you move up your body to your calves, knees, and thighs, note any tension and let it go.

4. Move up to your hips and slowly to your lower back. Slowly move your focus to your upper back and shoulders. Visualize any tension drifting away and being replaced with calm. Move to your chest and your shoulders. Be aware of how they feel as you tense and release your muscles.

5. Focus on your neck and head. Release any tension from each part of your face and your scalp. Move to your upper arms, your triceps, then your biceps, your forearms, your hands, and your fingers. Take slow, deep breaths.

6. After you've scanned your entire body, focus your awareness completely on your breath. Breathe in, slowly and deeply. Then breathe out fully. During each breath start counting very slowly backward from 5. 5...4...3... Between each number give yourself a sleepy suggestion, such as, *I will be asleep soon. My eyes are getting heavy. I feel my muscles getting heavy. My body is relaxed.*

7. When you catch yourself thinking about something instead of focusing on your breath, notice that it is happening, and start counting down again from 5. If you make it down to 1 a couple of times, you will soon be asleep. Good night.

Chapter 3

Conquering
Stressful Thoughts

This chapter addresses the ways mindfulness can neutralize many of the overpowering thoughts that create stress and trigger the body's physical reaction to stress.

The stress you feel stems from the way you interpret a situation. For example, imagine that you are a high-performing college student. You work hard, you are smart, and you expect to be the best in your class. After taking a test in one of the classes in your major, you find out that you earned a grade of only 75. How do you think you would feel? Ouch! The next day in class, you find out that the curve on that test was very low, and your 75 was actually an A. How do you think you would feel then?

You can see how your thoughts create the way you feel. Many of the thoughts that make you feel bad are misinterpretations and cause stress. The exercises in this chapter will show you the ways that mindfulness can distance you from the thoughts that create the stress.

1

Avoid
Thought Traps

Time

1 to 2 Minutes

Best for

Reducing stress-inducing thoughts

The cause of your stress is your thinking. Try to remember a time when you were stressed. For example, did your boss give you a last-minute project with a deadline of the exact time you had to pick up your child from school? What were your thoughts that created the stress? *I won't get the project finished in time. I won't be on time to pick up my child.* The truth is, you didn't know that you wouldn't be able to finish the report on time. You always had in the past. And you didn't know what your boss would say if you told him that your 6-year-old was waiting at school for you to pick him up. Yet the stress developed because you thought of the worst-case scenarios.

You fell into a "thought trap." These traps make you feel bad even though there is no proof that the thought you are having is completely true. Cognitive Behavioral Therapy (CBT) is the most effective therapy for changing thoughts that are not totally realistic but still make you feel bad. The cornerstone of this approach is based on what are called Cognitive Distortions. These are:

All-or-Nothing Thinking	You look at everything in terms of black and white.
Overgeneralization	You are going through something now, but you believe it will go on for the rest of your life.
Mental Lens	You do five things during the day, but you focus on the one that wasn't good, and that is all you see.
Discounting the Positive	You discount positive facts that contradict assumptions you make, or positive facts don't count.
Jumping to Conclusions	You come to a conclusion or a belief about something without having all the facts.
Magnification	You exaggerate the importance of your problem or shortcomings.
Emotional Reasoning	You assume that your negative emotions necessarily reflect the way things really are.
Should Statements	You tell yourself that things should be the way you hoped or expected them to be.
Labeling	You attach a negative label to yourself—a form of All-or-Nothing Thinking.
Personalization	You blame yourself or hold yourself accountable for something that you had no control over.

Feeling Good, The New Mood Therapy. Burns, D. Harper Collins. 1980

The key to avoiding these thinking traps is to realize that you are looking at a situation from one of these distorted perspectives. The following steps will free you from this burden.

1. Stop and ask yourself, *What am I thinking right now?*

2. Is the thought realistic or does it fit any of the Cognitive Distortion patterns? If it does fit one of those patterns, by definition, you cannot say the thought is definitely true.

3. Take a deep breath, focusing on the inhale and then the exhale. Remember that it is important to not get trapped in thoughts that are not realistic and that make you feel bad.

4. Stay focused on the present and be aware that you are simply having a thought.

5. Replace the thought with an alternative one you know is 100% true.

2

Stop, Look, and Listen

Time

5 Minutes

Best for

Staying objective in the moment

Unconscious bias exists and often directs your behavior without your knowledge, because it is *unconscious*. When you act in a biased manner, you often suffer consequences. All too often you might make an assumption about someone—whose hair is too long or too gray, or who pauses a little too long before answering a question—only to find out that your assumption was totally wrong. Mindfulness is a valuable tool in protecting you from these unintended consequences. It is about being in the moment, with no judgment and no expectation. When you are in the moment, you can experience the other person as he or she is. Being mindful in situations with others is an invaluable tool for you to be objective and to control the beliefs you may have and not even know about.

1. When going into a new situation, take slow, deep breaths and let your awareness expand. Because biases might not be conscious, you can protect yourself from them by being in the present and being fully aware and open. Focus on your breath. Then look around; what do you see?

2. Be aware of any instant thoughts about the person or people with whom you are meeting. If you do have an instant thought, stop, take a breath, and become open to your senses. Relax. Identify any judgmental thoughts, not just negative ones. You might be influenced in a positive but unrealistic way as well. If you find your mind jumping to a conclusion or making an assumption, stop. Get focused on the moment and stay in the present. Look at the thought without judgment.

3. Pay attention also to any emotions you feel. Do you have any hints of frustration or resentment? Do you feel disconnected? If so, try to focus back on your breath. Stay in the present and don't let your emotions influence your behavior.

4. Listen mindfully to the words the person is saying. What do they mean to you? How do you understand them? Stay focused on the sensations you experience.

5. Observe the person and register any thoughts that emerge. Again, notice these without judgment and be as objective as you can.

6. When you are receptive to another person, they will often be receptive to you in return. Observe any effort on their part to be responsive. You may be surprised by what you find.

3

Sharpen Your Focus

Time

10 Minutes

Best for

Tightening concentration

A number of studies have shown that mindfulness increases your ability to focus and concentrate. It makes logical sense: Mindfulness is the art of focusing. Using mindfulness to enhance your concentration is an exercise that sharpens your ability by giving you control over what you focus on. It is like tightening and loosening your grip of attention. Here, you will learn another tool for maintaining your focus in several different situations.

1. Find a comfortable place to sit. It could be outside or indoors.

2. Breathe deeply and slowly.

3. Find an object to focus on and simply watch it. If a thought comes into your mind, note it and then gently refocus on the object. The goal is to stay focused on one point. This will help you practice your control of attention.

4. Continue to breathe gently and deeply. Now slightly loosen your gaze around the object. Still keep it central, but look at a little of what is around it. It is like loosening your attention grip slightly to give you a wider view.

5. Now tighten your gaze back to the object.

6. Continue to do this for 5 minutes. You will find that you have control over what you focus on.

7. Now, change the focus to what is on the periphery of your vision. Do not strain your eyes, but notice what is to the left side and then to the right side, what is up and what is down.

8. When your attention drifts back to the center, gently bring your focus back to the periphery. Let yourself relax as you explore conscious control over your concentration.

9. Continue to do this for 5 minutes.

4

Open Awareness

Time

5 Minutes

Best for

Expanding your focus

You have explored mindfulness that focuses on breath, which is a solitary focus that is internally directed. Another version of mindfulness involves focusing on one sensation at a time before moving to another. A third type of mindfulness is open awareness, during which you focus on all the stimuli at the same time. I compare it to listening to music. Sometimes, one instrument's tones stand out and then you hear another one becoming dominant. Your focus shifts from the guitar riff to the drum solo, and then the bass gets your attention. You are loving the music and paying attention to the different components. Open awareness is like listening to all the instruments at the same time. This exercise takes practice, and it gives you another way to stay present in the moment. When paying attention to all your senses, you may notice that you will want to shut down and that your focus narrows down to one input at a time. If that happens, be aware of it and gradually open to any other inputs that you can.

1. Sit in a quiet place. Breathe slowly in and out through your nose. Be aware of the sensations of your breath. Notice the warmth. Feel the air going into your lungs. Feel your chest expand. Do this three times.

2. As you focus on your breath, look straight ahead. What do you see? Is it stationary or is it moving? Instead of shifting your focus as you become aware of another sensation, focus on your breath and on what you see at the same time. Feel the expansion of your awareness.

3. Now turn your head. While remaining conscious of your breath, feel the rotation of your neck and also see what you are looking at. Hear whatever sounds come into awareness.

4. Feel sensations in your hands and fingers along with the other inputs. How are you sitting? Do thoughts come into your head? It is as if you are at a giant traffic intersection, and you want to keep track of all the cars, the vegetation, the signs, and the road.

5. Keep breathing slowly and describe what it's like. You might feel expansive. You might feel that it is too much to keep track of. Let yourself be as open as you can.

6. As you continue, identify any other sensations, like the pressure on your back or the feeling in your arms. Try to expand your consciousness as much as you can for 5 minutes. You will feel more open.

5

Visualize This

Time

10 Minutes

Best for

Achieving your goals

In life, it is difficult to score a point if you don't have a target. Visualization helps you develop what you want to shoot for. It also shapes it. Some believe that to achieve anything you need to rehearse a mental image every day, to condition your mind to accept that reality. This exercise is to help you realize your aspirations and achieve your goals, which do not have to be only material ones. You can also visualize yourself being kinder or more generous.

1. Pick a time each day that you will dedicate to your visualization. Choose the specific goal you wish to visualize.

2. Write out specifically what you want to happen. Include as much detail as you can. Let's say you want a new car. Choose the exact model and all the extras.

3. In addition to identifying the end goal, think about the characteristics that will help you achieve it. The car will cost money. What are the personality characteristics you will need to get the money to get the car? Write those down specifically. Keep your goal in mind. For example, *I will do whatever it takes to win. I am determined. I am dedicated. I will not stop until I am stopped. I will sacrifice other expenses to get my car.*

4. Find a quiet place to sit comfortably. Slowly start to breathe in and out through your nose. Feel the sensations in your body as you relax. Let all your senses come to life.

5. Now picture the car with you in it. See yourself starting the engine every morning and accelerating onto the highway. Continue visualizing this image for 5 minutes. Now picture the self you will be to accomplish getting the car. Visualize being determined, being dedicated, being tireless.

6. In addition to your morning visualization, read your visualization several times each day. Stay focused on the goal as you read. Take slow, deep breaths. Continue to perform these exercises until you achieve each goal visualized.

6

Mind of
an Athlete

Time

5 Minutes

**Best
for**

**Improving
your game**

Many professional athletes report that visualization is an important part of their practice, results in more success, and allows them to conquer stressful thoughts in all areas of their lives. Golfers rehearse seeing the putt go into the hole before they swing. Baseball players visualize hitting a curve ball or experiencing the contact of the bat on a home run ball. If you enjoy participating in sports, you can try this exercise to improve your game.

1. Let your body relax and pay attention to any sensations in the moment.

2. While staying centered, start creating the visualization. Spend time mentally rehearsing and focusing on the exact skills you need. If you are a golfer, visualize the perfect drive, visualize yourself with perfect form, and watch the ball fly in a perfect arc. Repeat this on different days with your iron shots and with your putts. Picture every detail. If you play tennis, visualize yourself hitting the perfect serve. You want to see your every move. Do the same with any sport you play.

3. End the activity seeing yourself as victorious. Feel the feeling of having won.

4. Practice this as many times each day as you can.

7

Affirming Yourself

Time

30 minutes initially, 30 seconds 40 times each day afterward

Best for

Achieving your dreams

Affirmations are intended to reset unconscious negative thoughts. The theory (we believe it is much more than just a theory!) is that when you first start saying your positive affirmations, they may not be true, but with repetition they sink into your subconscious mind, you start to believe them, and eventually they become your reality. They become a self-fulfilling prophecy.

1. Start by sitting quietly and writing down your affirmations. Take slow, deep breaths and open yourself to all your senses. Stay focused and centered.

2. Think about what is important to you and what you want to happen in the future. Pay attention to any thoughts that emerge while staying relaxed and receptive. Let the ideas flow from you. Do not think actively, but be aware of the qualities, goals, and future you want to attain. Do you want more financial success? Do you want a relationship? Would you like to feel more confidence? Consider as many dimensions as you can.

3. Write your first affirmation about some of your strengths. For example, if you want to achieve a goal that will take a lot of work, you may write, *I am tireless. I am determined. I am dauntless.* Capture the essence of the strengths that will drive your success.

4. Write another affirmation about the end result. For example, *I am achieving my specific goal,* or *I am finishing the paper that I am writing,* or *I am getting the promotion.* Continue to breathe slowly, staying focused on your breath and any other sensations.

5. Now write an affirmation that will help you reach your personal goal, like getting into better shape or losing weight. For example, *I am in total control of what I eat.* As you do this, maintain a focused and mindful stance.

6. Write other affirmations about feeling excited and energized, about finding love, about advancing professionally, about being a better parent.

7. Read your affirmations every day, 20 times in the morning and 20 times at night. It is imperative that you do this every day, weekends included. As you read your affirmations, stay open and focused. You are reprogramming your mind to work for you in a different way, one that can change your life.

FLIPPING THE SCRIPT

Your beliefs form from the combination of your experiences. When you have been disappointed or discouraged, you can develop an expectation that the same things will happen when you seek them. It feels as though you never achieve the result you want. Unconsciously, you then act to meet that expectation. That ends up with you giving up on getting the circumstances that you want. You can reverse the pattern with a combination of powerful affirmations that are specific and focused with conscious visualizations. When you replace those beliefs, you start changing the unwritten script. Practicing this combination every day with full intention can position you to attain your goal. It is as if you attract the result you want.

8

Let It Be

Time

5 Minutes

Best for

Self-acceptance

Accepting your life and your feelings is vital to being in the present. When you do not accept an emotion, it stays active in your mind and creates stress. Do not confuse acceptance with resignation. Accepting something does not mean you are passive and help-less. The following exercise will help you learn the art of accepting the emotions that accompany situa-tions you wish were different.

1. When you are facing a difficult or unhappy emotion, start by identifying that you are feeling bad. Notice the physical cues that occur when you feel bad.

2. Breathe slow, deep breaths and focus on your existence in this moment. Be aware of what you hear, or see, or smell. Let yourself stay very present.

3. When a thought or the thought that is hard to take comes into your mind, just watch it. See it as a thought and watch yourself having the thought. Do not let it go around and around. There is a difference between being in the thought and watching it. For example, let us say you find out that a friend who has a similar job to yours just received a promotion. Your thought might be, *He is better than I am*, or *I will never be successful*.

4. Be aware of the emotion. Look at the thought as simply a thought instead of believing that you are inferior. You do not need to feel bad about it. Don't judge it. Don't fight it. You are just having a thought. Instead of attaching meaning to the thought, stay unattached.

5. Keep focused on your breath. If the thought stays there, keep watching it. If it moves on, stay focused on your body.

9

Know Your Strengths

Time

5 Minutes

Best for

Maximizing your potential

People who know their strengths and use them frequently tend to feel happier and have better self-esteem and are more likely to accomplish their goals. However, many people have a hard time identifying their strengths. They see their traits as ordinary, even when they are not. This exercise will help you tap in to your strengths and articulate your abilities.

1. Start by sitting in a comfortable position in a quiet place. Take slow, deep breaths, focusing on your breath and any sensations.

2. Let your mind wander to consider the best things about you. What have you appreciated about yourself in the past week? Notice if any images come up. Sometimes, you may not see anything that you appreciate. Think back to any time in the last year when you were happy about something you did or felt.

3. Still focusing on your breath, ask yourself, what was the most pleasing interaction with someone this past week? What did you do that you were proud of? If you can't think of anything from the recent week, think back to the past. On days when you are feeling down, it may be more difficult, but go back in time if you need to.

4. Make a list of everything you think of.

5. After you make your list, choose five close friends or work colleagues and ask them to tell you what your strengths are.

6. Compare their observations with your own. Which ones make sense to you? Choose one of these strengths and think of at least one way you can use it in the coming week.

10

Oh
Happy Day

Time

5 Minutes

*Best
for*

**Feeling
positive**

Gratitude helps us remember what is good in our lives. Think of how much time you spend reliving the past or worrying about the future. When you replace those thoughts with thoughts of good things that have happened, you generate a greater sense of happiness. It is too easy to take wonderful things in your life for granted. In this exercise, I will show you how to harness gratitude to your full advantage and thereby reduce stress.

1. Start by sitting in a comfortable position in a quiet place.

2. Focus on the moment, taking in all sensory experiences and keeping your mind very still. Say, *For this I am grateful.* You are being grateful for being alive, for breathing, for being able to feel.

3. Now bring into awareness one person, event, experience, or anything about which you can be grateful. Repeat *For this I am grateful.* Don't just say the words. Let yourself feel the good feelings that accompany the thought. Think of the person in detail. What are you thankful for when you think of them?

4. As you concentrate on feeling thankful, breathe deeply, and feel yourself fill with gratitude.

5. Focus now on yourself. Find one thing you love about yourself. Say, *For this I am grateful.* Think of a person who truly cares about you; what do they love about you? Say, *For this I am grateful.*

6. Think of one situation yesterday that made you feel grateful. Say again, *For this I am grateful.*

ATTITUDES OF GRATITUDE

The following are ways to maintain an attitude of gratitude throughout the days, months, and years.

Keep a gratitude journal. Every other day, write an entry about anything you were thankful for over the past two days.

Keep a gratitude jar. Get a medium-size storage jar. Decorate it in happy, whimsical tones. At the end of each day, write three things you were grateful for that day, and place them in the jar.

Every night before sleep, think of one more thing or person for which you are thankful.

Chapter 4

Overcoming Stressful Emotions

This chapter will show you how to use mindfulness to conquer difficult, stressful emotions and unproductive, out-of-control emotional responses. The gift of mindfulness is that it allows you to be apart from the emotions that so often drive your behavior or push you to react to the behavior of others.

Emotions are healthy and an important piece of our coping and response apparatus. Difficult emotions occur automatically when there is danger or something to be afraid of. Sadness occurs in response to a loss, and anger in response to frustration. When not acknowledged and handled the right way, these responses create stress, and stress affects emotions.

In today's society, most people are not taught how to deal with their emotions and end up being afraid of them. If someone is angry, it feels dangerous. If you are angry, you might feel unsafe. If you are envious, you will feel unhappy without any positive outcome.

This exercises in this chapter will help you identify your feelings. They will show you how to allow and accept them. They will also help you control them. Your emotions are alive in the way you are alive, and appreciating them is one of the most important things you can do to reduce stress.

1

Feelings Have a Name

Time

5 Minutes

Best for

Handling emotions

If you grew up in an emotional household, you probably know what you are feeling. If you grew up in a home where emotions were frowned upon or not allowed, you might not know what they are. This exercise is designed to help you identify your emotions. The range of emotions are happiness, sadness, fear, and anger. Happiness feels good. Fear, anger, and sadness don't feel so good. To identify emotions when you are not used to them, you need to connect a situation with the way you felt inside. Identifying the physical cues to your emotions is a powerful way to know what you are feeling and will help you have more control over how you respond. Once you become aware of your emotions and realize that they are safe, you will find that they can be a great asset.

1. Think back to any time when you saw someone who was important to you, perhaps your child or a loved one, after not seeing her for a week or even a day. What were the sensations in your body? Did your heart take a small leap? Did your breathing become slightly more rapid? Did you break into a smile? That would be happiness.

2. Think of being in a very frustrating situation. Perhaps you rushed to get to the supermarket before it closed because you needed something for your child's lunch the next day, and they locked the door just before you arrived. What were the physical signs? Did you feel tension in your back or shoulder blades? Did you feel hot and flustered? Did you feel angry?

3. Breathe deeply. Let the air go deep down into your lungs.

4. Think now of a time when you were really frightened. Perhaps a mouse ran across the kitchen floor, or you got a flat tire on a rainy night. Or think of another time when your child was late returning home. We can assume that was fear. You might have felt a chill down your spine or had cold hands.

5. Reflect on a time when you lost someone, a parent or a loved one, who meant a lot to you. Perhaps a beloved pet died. What were the physical signs that occurred? Did you want to withdraw? Did you want to cry? Did you just want someone to be there with you?

6. These are emotions. They can be powerful. They can be uncomfortable. When you feel them, try to identify what kind of emotion you feel by using your physical reactions as guides. If you are not accustomed to using your emotions as a tool, try to think of them as serving a purpose. Then figure out what purpose they serve.

2

Letting It All Out

Time

5 Minutes

Best for

Avoiding the problems that occur when feelings are not expressed

When you have difficult emotions such as anger, fear, and anxiety, you may not want to face them because they are uncomfortable. After you identify them, it is important to acknowledge them in a nonjudgmental manner. It is *normal* to feel emotions. They are a vibrant part of being alive. When you don't allow yourself to feel your emotions, they often translate into a physical problem such as high blood pressure, headaches, or muscular tension. These steps will help you accept the normal reactions your body creates in response to situations. The purpose of this exercise is to train yourself to experience an emotion rather than block it out.

1. Start by sitting or lying in a comfortable position in a quiet place. Take slow, deep breaths. Let yourself go into a relaxed state, with all your senses open.

2. Now picture the last time you were angry or anxious. Do you remember the physical sensations you felt? It's not comfortable to have those feelings. What were you angry about? As you think of the situation, visualize the anger. Rather than becoming angry again, try to see that you had an angry reaction.

3. As you do this, see the anger as a response to a specific situation. Rather than saying *I am angry*, say, *I see the emotion of anger.* Rather than being angry, say, *I see the emotion of anger.*

4. Now think of a time when you felt afraid or anxious.

5. Try to recreate the scene in your mind. Picture every detail of the situation and your place in it. Think of what you were wearing. Take a deep breath. Let yourself relax and be open and picture any sensations you had. The reason for doing this is to be able to recognize that you are having feelings the next time it occurs.

6. You may find that by heightening your awareness, you will be more aware of the emotion the next time you experience it. If you feel an emotion, identify that you are feeling it. Then take a breath, center yourself, and let yourself be open to anything else you experience. Pay attention to your physical reactions and to thoughts that arise.

7. Wait until the next time you are anxious or afraid. When you are, breathe and stay focused on your sensations. Identify the cues that tell you that you are anxious or angry. Watch them, feel them, and identify your emotion.

8. Consider all your options to handle the situation. The main point is that you do not need to avoid and run away from the emotion. Let yourself experience the feeling.

3

Watch, Don't Judge

Time

5 Minutes

Best for

Staying in the present when uncomfortable

When you have uncomfortable or difficult feelings, it is natural to want to avoid facing them. Often, we are trained to ignore them. "Don't cry," "Don't be angry," "Don't feel sad," "Don't be weak." Although commonly heard, these phrases create a problem because having feelings is a normal part of being human.

Another reason you may not want to feel a bad feeling is that you think you need to do something in response to the feeling. However, feeling angry does not mean you have to beat someone up. Feeling sad does not mean you have to stay at home and disappear from the world. Learning to tolerate the existence of an emotion is critical to being realistically in the present.

In previous exercises, you learned how to identify unpleasant emotions and stop them from taking over. Now, I will show you how to allow yourself to feel them.

1. Whenever you find yourself in an emotionally loaded situation and your uncomfortable emotions build and your mind starts racing, take several slow, deep breaths. Open yourself to your senses.

2. Focus on any physical sensations. Notice them without judgment, and think about the situation in which you are disappointed or upset. Be aware of and identify any emotions that emerge.

3. Now watch these emotions as if you are standing across the room from them and looking at them without judgment. This is what I call the third-person defense. Rather than being part of the emotionally charged interaction, you can look at it as an observer. As the one watching, you become able to separate yourself from your emotional reactions.

4. By observing the scene from across the room you can observe yourself in the situation and think of the different ways you might handle it. For example, if in a disagreement with Jane: "Jane is not listening to what Mary is saying. Mary is getting frustrated. What are the ways Mary can handle this?"

5. Watch the emotion as if it were an object that did not influence you.

6. Continue to breathe and stay centered. Keep in mind that you don't have to do anything just because you are having an emotion. Simply watch.

UNDERSTANDING YOUR EMOTIONS

Human emotions have remained the same throughout evolution and are connected to complex physical responses to situations. When you are afraid or angry, your body produces a range of hormones including adrenaline and noradrenaline. These activate the body's ability to escape or stay safe from an attack

4

Unbottle Your Emotions

Time

5 Minutes

Best for

Preventing symptoms that come from suppressing emotion

The human is a complex being. If you look at other species in the animal kingdom, you do not see them denying difficult feelings, suppressing them, or doing anything other than feeling them and expressing them. If you try to take a bone away while a dog is chewing on it, even the gentlest dog might bare his teeth and growl aggressively and, if you go further, bite you. That dog is angry and has no inhibition about expressing it. On the other hand, if you are uncomfortable with anger and someone does something that makes you angry, you might not acknowledge it; you might just bite your tongue and say nothing. Then, you might go home with a terrible headache and be unable to sleep; your blood pressure would go up, and you would spend the next four weeks ruminating about what you wish you had said. To express emotions, you can speak to another person, or if that is not possible because of your comfort level, you can express how you feel to yourself.

1. After you have been in an emotional situation, sit quietly and breathe deeply in and out through your nose. Pay attention to any physical sensations. Let yourself be calm.

2. If you start having an angry emotion, look for any physical cues. Notice if your chest gets tight or if you become very tense. If you are not used to or are uncomfortable with anger, you will have physical reactions but may not understand that it is anger.

3. Look for signs of being anxious or frightened. Your stomach may feel like it is sinking or you may get an upset stomach. You might feel tingling.

4. Being happy is an emotion, too. Notice signs of feeling joyful.

5. When you are angry, start to express it by telling yourself that you are angry. Then take a sheet of paper and write about the incident that upset you. Pay attention to the details of where you were and what you were doing.

6. Describe what your response was, and now write how you would have liked to respond.

7. If you were anxious, think of someone with whom you can share your responses. If that is not possible, identify the thoughts you were getting anxious about. Write down the likelihood of that event occurring. When you are anxious, you may not link your emotion to the probability of it happening.

8. Return to your breath and focus on your internal state. Let any feelings drift away.

5

Acts of Kindness— to Yourself

Time

5 minutes each morning

Best for

Softening your emotions

In addition to the mindfulness methods you have learned to avoid or relieve stress, I want to address one more thing you can do for yourself. That is to take care of yourself. Despite the hectic life you lead and all the responsibilities you have, you can soften your life. Today's world is very hectic—fast paced and success driven. You most likely are running at top speed from the time you wake until you go to sleep. You also probably do not reserve any time when you can simply physically stop. Earlier in this book, I mentioned that the first stage of stress is helpful in dealing with the stressful situation. Normally, the situation passes and the stress response returns to normal. When the stress continues, however, you stay on high alert, and that can create physical and psychological problems. You can counter those effects by being kind to yourself during the day.

You can schedule the five-minute miracle by taking five-minute breaks between running from one errand to another or from one meeting to another. You can stop to have a coffee and smell the aroma. You can get yourself a treat. Think of two small luxuries you can give yourself every day. We hardly ever examine our schedule to see how it can be broken up. We tend to just ram through the day, rather than plan it with time for ourselves built in. Think about how you can make your day a friendlier and kinder one.

1. Start your day by getting up 5 minutes earlier.

2. Find a quiet place and breathe deeply. Concentrate on letting tension go. Open yourself to your senses and be centered. Pay attention to any sensations.

3. Think of all you have to do that day, or look at your calendar, and find times and places where you can schedule 5-minute breaks. Write these in your calendar as if they were appointments.

4. Write down a list of possible small nice things you can do for yourself.

5. Plan time during the day to do at least two of them.

6. Choose a number of your favorite songs that you can play during the day when you go out or during your commute to and from work. Then play them.

7. Think of any other activity you find pleasurable. Figure out how to fit it into your schedule and then do it.

8. Finally, plan something relaxing to do before you go to bed. Remember: You are important.

6

Getting Grounded

Time

5 Minutes

Best for

Handling intense anxiety

Grounding essentially means getting in touch with reality when your mind is taking off. It is the ability to detach from overwhelming feelings and be fully present during the immediate moment. If you are someone who experiences anxiety on a regular basis, there might be times when your anxiety overpowers your rational thought. If you were a victim of a previous trauma, as in PTSD, for example, it can come flooding back with flashbacks or intense memories. Drug cravings or self-harm impulses can also make you feel like you have no control. When this happens, your mind takes over your sense of reality. You may not be able to see a more realistic picture, and anxiety controls your reason. This can be very scary, and you must connect to reality as soon as you can. The most fundamental way to do this is to touch something real.

1. Take several slow, deep breaths. It is okay to sit or stand. If you are sitting, firmly grasp the arms of the chair. Make contact with it so you really feel it. If you are standing, stomp your foot on the ground to feel the contact.

2. Touch your face. Feel the contact.

3. If you are indoors, touch the walls. If you are outdoors, find something else to touch, such as a tree or car.

4. Listen to sounds. Turn up the radio or stereo.

5. Access your other senses. Find something to taste, such as a strong mint or a pepper. Feel the harshness of it.

6. Look around and orient yourself. Where are you? What day is it? Give yourself the answer out loud. Take some more breaths and stay in the present.

7

Handling the Tornado

Time

5 Minutes

Best
for

**Reacting to
your emotions
in a controlled
manner**

In some instances you may have difficulty controlling your emotions. You may have temper outbursts that create disturbances and get you in trouble. You may feel that you have no control over your anxiety. When your emotions are out of control, you probably feel helpless and unable to change your responses, which may be disruptive or inappropriate.

The major key to overcoming stressful emotions is to see when they are happening, before the progression of a strong emotion is a trigger. When you start experiencing the physical signs of emotion, identify what emotion you are feeling. By identifying the emotion first instead of reacting to it, you can interpret the meaning of the situation to which you are reacting. Finally, you can react in a responsive and thoughtful manner. In order to remain not controlled by the emotion, you can intervene at any of these three points. The process of identifying the emotion gives you time before you react. You can then adjust your behavior accordingly.

1. Immediately pay attention to the physical cues that signal a strong emotion, like a flushed face, a rapid heartbeat, a sinking feeling.

2. Take a slow, deep breath, and open yourself to your senses. Try to put yourself in a relaxed state. Stay in the present moment and allow yourself to feel what is happening in your body. If there is tension in your muscles or back, notice it as tension.

3. Identify the emotions. If you feel anger, you need to press the *pause* button and withdraw from the situation long enough to consider your options of responding.

4. Identify to yourself that you are having a strong emotion, and that emotion wants to control you, and you cannot let it.

5. Be alert for any thoughts or triggers that might further upset you, and continue to breathe slowly and deeply as these triggers occur. Be aware of your surroundings. Identify the thoughts driving the emotion.

6. Cognitive Distortions (page 33) can make you misinterpret events. See if any of these are influencing your perceptions. If they are, replace them with more accurate ones. Examples are: Jumping to Conclusions, where you think you know what someone else is thinking, and Mental Lens, where you focus on one negative event and discount any others that were positive.

7. Continue breathing, slowly focusing on your physical sensations, staying centered and open.

MINDFULNESS EXPLAINED

It is important to understand that mindfulness is not the same as psychotherapy. Mindfulness teaches you how to detach from the thoughts that create stress. Cognitive therapy gives you the tools to defeat the thoughts that create stress. Cognitive therapy was developed by Dr. Aaron Beck in the late 1960s. In 1980, Dr. David Burns expanded the approach and wrote *Feeling Good, the New Mood Therapy.*

8

Let It All Out

Time

10 Minutes

Best for

Letting out pent-up anger

Studies show that holding in your angry feelings can have detrimental effects on both your physical and mental health. Repressed or suppressed stress and anger are associated with higher rates of depression as well as physical problems such as high blood pressure, headaches, and stomach problems. In this exercise, I'll guide you through a healthy practice of expressing your emotions. There are several methods to letting out your aggressive feelings. You can identify them and express them by screaming or hitting something harmless. You can identify them and visualize them blowing up and being pulverized. Lastly, you can identify them, notice that they are angry feelings, and let them float away. Whichever you choose, remember to do what feels comfortable.

1. Pay attention to the physical cues of being angry. One of the most important elements of expressing anger is to know it is there. Sometimes when you are angry, just identifying that and saying to yourself that you are angry can be enough to release it.

2. Another way to let it go is to visualize it. After identifying a situation in which you are angry, take a deep breath. At some point, find a quiet place and sit comfortably, close your eyes, and breathe long, deep breaths while you focus on any sensory experiences.

3. Observe the anger as a roiling mass. Give it a color. Let it spin and roll. Express how frustrated you have been, watch it, and now send it away. Let it drift away.

4. Now come back to focusing on the present through the breath.

5. Alternatively, you can try a more primal method. Go to a private place and think of the situation about which you are mad.

6. Scream at the top of your lungs until you are tired. You can also punch a pillow or something that will not hurt your hand. After you are tired, see if you feel differently.

9

Creating Positivity

Time

**5 minutes
three times
each day**

**Best
for**

**Being in a
good mood
and being
healthy**

Feeling positive has a component of doing things that are upbeat. It also is controlled by how you look at a situation, which affects how you feel. Very often people find the negative in a situation rather than the positive, seeing the glass half empty. There are reasons for this, such as not getting your hopes up to avoid later disappointment, but whatever the reason, thinking negatively becomes a pattern that becomes a habit. You can change that pattern by finding the positive side rather than the negative. The way to change a habit is to replace the old behavior with the new one and practice doing that every time.

1. First thing in the morning, do something nice for yourself. It could be getting a good cup of coffee. It might be a warm shower, or anything else you enjoy.

2. Think one happy thought.

3. Sit quietly and open yourself to all your senses. Breathe slowly and deeply while focusing on your physical sensations. Stay as much in the moment as possible. Focus on one thing that has made you feel good in the last day or week.

4. Practice looking at glasses half full instead of half empty. You can feel good or bad depending on how you look at a situation. Practice seeing the positive. This is a pattern that requires practice, and you need to do it at every opportunity.

5. Use the Smile and Hello practice developed by Dr. David Burns. As you are walking down the street, make eye contact with a person (preferably not under headphones) and smile. You will always get a smile back.

6. If you start feeling down in any way, identify the thought. Let yourself feel that. Think about what you might do about the situation. If there is nothing you can do, let the feeling pass by and focus on something else.

7. Play an upbeat song you like. Keep songs that uplift you stored on your phone so you can access them at will.

10

Don't Worry, Be Happy

Time

5 Minutes

Best for

Making your life feel good

Happiness is one of the keys to life. It has been related to living longer, having more satisfying relationships, and being more resilient. Also, it is a choice to be happy or not. There are two ways to make yourself happy. One is to pursue activities that bring joy into your life. The other is to stop doing whatever you are doing that makes you unhappy. This exercise helps you learn some of the skills to be happier. The elements of happiness are gratefulness and appreciation for what you have rather than what you don't have. Also, a positive outlook boosts your level of happiness. Optimists are more resilient and more successful. If you do not usually look at the bright side, you may have a habit that needs to be changed. Changing a habit is accomplished by learning a new pattern to replace the habitual one you use. Then you have to practice the new pattern over and over. Relatively quickly the new pattern will form a new habit that becomes primary. In following these steps, if any make you feel good, keep practicing them.

1. Decide to be happy. You may not realize yet that this is a choice, but make a conscious choice that when you have two ways of looking at something or feeling good or feeling bad, make the choice to feel good.

2. Start by sitting in a comfortable position in a quiet place. Breathe deeply in and out through your nose. Feel your breath. Focus on any sensations you become aware of. While in a relaxed state, picture a point of happiness within you. Let it have life and see it grow. Picture it flowing through your body and filling you with the feeling and sense of happiness. Do this step every morning.

3. Find two times during the day to think of something you are grateful for.

4. The next time you feel discouraged or think pessimistically, reverse the assumption and replace it with a positive expectation. Think that you can do something rather than that you can't, even if it might take a longer time or require more effort. If you are taking a test, catch yourself if your starting belief is that you will fail. Reverse the expectation.

5. When you find yourself thinking negatively about another person, find their positive qualities. Replace your negative interpretations and assumptions with positive ones. Think of how you can interpret their behavior differently.

6. Find a new friend. Pay attention if you cross paths with someone who could become a new friend. Many studies have shown that relationships are an important part of being happy.

Chapter 5

Reducing Stressful Communication

Mindfulness is a powerful tool for reducing the frustration, irritation, or annoyance that can occur in certain communications. Mindful communication can also enhance your ability to connect with others in a meaningful way.

Do you ever get distracted when you are talking with someone and realize that you don't remember anything that was said? Do you ever find yourself prejudging what someone else is saying or that you are in your own head judging yourself? Those actions block communication. By staying mindful, you have the advantage of truly being in the moment.

Interacting with people is your door to being successful. It is the key to making contact in a meaningful way. By staying focused, you maximize your abilities. There are so many thoughts that clog our brains. Taking mindfulness with you wherever you go gives you the advantage.

In this chapter, you will learn how to make whomever you are communicating with feel understood and truly heard. You also will learn to bring awareness to the way you communicate so that you get your points across more effectively. Finally, you will gain a greater sense of how you can interact in ways that make you feel great.

1

Mindful Listening

Time

5 Minutes

Best for

Connected communication

It is often said that when truly successful people are speaking with you, it feels like no one else is in the room. Their attention is so complete that you feel entranced. Such is the power of mindful listening. When you can integrate the balanced, nonjudgmental openness of mindfulness with the act of listening, you make a person feel truly heard. Paying complete attention is difficult, though, particularly if what is being said is disagreeable or uninteresting to you. This exercise will show you the art of listening mindfully.

1. Make a conscious decision to listen mindfully during your next conversation. Your goal is to listen as you stay in the present.

2. Observe the other person. Focus on the words spoken and think of what they are trying to communicate. If you find your mind wandering, bring it back to the present. Rather than thinking about what you are going to say, hear what the other person is saying.

3. If you don't agree with what the other person is saying, identify that and try to understand their point while staying open. If you feel an emotion, don't react. Pay attention to the physical cues, and notice that you are feeling something. Take a breath and focus on your senses. Get present in the moment. Recognize the emotion and bring your awareness back to your breathing.

4. Check in with the person to see if you are getting what they are saying. Repeat what you heard, but put it into your own words. What can you learn from the conversation?

5. Try to keep eye contact with the person who is speaking. Do not interrupt the speaker. Periodically, ask yourself what they meant. If you catch yourself daydreaming, come back to the conversation.

6. Try not to assume you know what the speaker is going to say; continue listening.

7. Organize what you learned, and ask questions to further enhance that knowledge. Encourage the speaker by acknowledging and nodding. You can even say, *Tell me more.* Show interest.

8. Pause before responding. Integrate what you heard the person say, think about it, then respond. Always let the speaker finish their sentence. Do not assume you know the ending. You must continue to concentrate. If you catch yourself getting distracted, bring yourself back to focus.

9. See if there is a difference in the way you feel when you have this type of dialogue.

2

Get It Off Your Mind

Time

5 Minutes

Best for

Getting your point across

There are two levels of communication: the words spoken and the emotions felt. The way you feel is much louder. Mindful speaking is being aware of all the levels on which you are communicating. It is not just important for clear communication, but it can also directly affect the result of the communication. Mindfulness allows you to be fully open to an experience. It also lets you be without judgment and accept things as they occur. This exercise will help you integrate mindfulness with what you want to say.

1. The next time you start to have a conversation, identify your intention to yourself. What do you want to get from the interchange? Do you want information? Do you want to make plans? Do you want to influence someone's decision?

2. To start, take a deep breath and open your senses. Quietly focus on your breathing, staying centered and in the present moment.

3. Before responding to the other person, pay attention to what they are saying and to any feelings that may arise for you. Then quickly monitor what you want to say. Try to see yourself from the outside. What is your motivation? What point are you trying to make? Are you asking for something? Do you want to influence something? By keeping your emotions to the side, you can make a better-informed response.

4. When listening to the other person, finish listening to what they are saying before you start thinking about your answer. If you get distracted or bored while listening, note that and come back to the conversation. Keep your intention in mind. Be aware of the impact of what you are saying.

5. Avoid the temptation to share your own story and talk only about yourself. Do not immediately offer advice when the other person describes a problem. They might just want to talk about it to get their thoughts straight.

6. Do not try to impress the other person.

7. If you find yourself responding to feelings that the person generated, stay as open and nonjudgmental as possible, and watch your reactions as if watching yourself from across the room. Stay centered and decide the best things to say.

8. Before the end of the interaction, check back to see if you accomplished your objective.

3

Conscious Conversation

Time

10 Minutes

Best for

Getting more of what you want

Think of a time when you wanted to convince someone to do something, or a time when you and your partner were arguing. What makes those situations difficult? It is probably that you or the other person don't feel understood.

Have you noticed that if someone wants something from you and is thinking only of themselves, you don't want to give them what they're asking for? Have you noticed that when you want something from someone and are thinking only of yourself, you don't get what you need? In this section, you'll learn how to listen and communicate more mindfully so that you can get more of what you want and give more consciously.

1. In any interaction, stay focused. Concentrate on your slow breathing. If in an argument, a dispute, or a negotiation, it is critical to be totally present. It is easy to get emotional and reactive, but those behaviors often prevent communication.

2. Pay attention to physical sensations, and pay attention to thoughts that wander; bring them back into focus.

3. Put yourself in the other person's shoes. When you start the conversation, think of what you want to accomplish, and continue to breathe and stay in the present.

4. Spot any emotions, like anger or resentment, that take your focus away from your effective communication. Again, think of what you would be thinking if you were the other person.

5. Use the 5 Secrets of Successful Communication developed by Dr. David Burns in *Feeling Good Together: The Secret to Making Troubled Relationships Work*. Find something to agree with in the other person's statement, summarize what you hear them saying, guess at what you think they are feeling, inquire to see if they have more to say, share your own feeling directly in that moment, and then find something nice to say about them.

6. As the other person makes a point, don't react. Listen carefully to the words they say, while paying full attention. It is important to hear the words without judgment and without reaction.

4

Understanding the Other Point of View

Time

5 Minutes

Best for

Cultivating empathy and understanding

You will succeed more in communicating or negotiating effectively if you understand the other person's point of view. Sometimes, particularly if you are emotional about a topic, it is conceptually difficult to do this. To practice how to respond, it can be helpful to role-play the situation by yourself or sometimes with another person. Let's use the example of you wanting a raise at your job but being anxious about asking for it.

1. Place two chairs opposite each other. Sit in one and start as yourself thinking about the conversation. Pay attention to the tension, if any, related to the fear of confrontation. You don't want to start a problem. Taking a breath, open yourself up to your senses. Continue to focus on your breath.

2. Picture your boss sitting in the other chair. Build in as much detail as you can. Think of how they are dressed. See the expression on their face. Now, while role-playing, go through the exercise of saying what you want.

3. Pay attention to even the subtlest of your feelings. Are you anxious, scared, resentful, or do you feel nothing?

4. Switch chairs. Now play the role of your boss. Try to put yourself in their shoes. What are they thinking about giving you a raise? Based on anything you know or have heard before, is there anything you can deduce? Staying focused on both your centered self and the thinking, can you think of a way to understand what their objections might be, or do you think they might be in favor of rewarding you?

5. To the extent that you can, picture how they might feel. What would they say? How does that feel to you? Switch chairs and respond. When answering, keep their position in mind. Continue switching chairs as you explore all the possible answers.

6. Role-playing is a good way to understand someone else's position and to find a way to bring it closer to yours, because you can rehearse saying what you need to say. You can do this by yourself or with another person.

5

Hold On
a Minute

Time

5 Minutes

Best for

Interpersonal matters

Have there been times you reacted without thinking and then were embarrassed? Were there times when you lost your temper and got in trouble? Studies have shown that those who can assess a situation and respond thoughtfully have more success and fewer consequences than their counterparts. This exercise will show you how you can gain greater effectiveness and control by responding rather than reacting.

As you go through your day, stay focused and centered by consciously breathing and staying aware of the present moment. When you face an interpersonal matter, or if someone asks you for a decision about something, start with a breath, and mindfully hear what the person is asking for.

1. Scan yourself quickly to identify any physical cues about how you are reacting, and identify any emotions you feel. By seeing that these sensations and emotions exist, you can detach them from your decision-making process. Look at the request from more than one angle. What are the consequences of your decision? Are there advantages and disadvantages? Which are greater? Now decide how to respond.

2. If someone says something hostile to you or acts in an aggressive manner, identify that it is happening. Take a breath and center yourself.

3. Recognize what the other person is doing: They are acting aggressively.

4. Look for signs of any emotions you are having and set those aside, then look at the different ways you might respond. There are usually more than one.

5. To use this technique, look at the interaction between you and the other person as though you were standing across the room observing the interchange. Then, as though you were advising yourself, think of your different options for responding.

6

Critical Curiosity

Time

5 Minutes

Best for

Deepening your understanding of new topics

Critical curiosity is one aspect of learning. It is characterized by the nonacceptance of the surface explanation of a subject. It means questioning a topic to allow for deeper knowledge. To be truly curious, you need to have an open mind. Geniuses like Einstein and Steve Jobs never stopped at the accepted destination.

The characteristics of mindfulness allow for critical curiosity. To be properly curious, you must be open and nonjudgmental, with no preconceived conclusions. Bringing curiosity to your mindfulness practice is especially helpful. With curiosity, mindfulness automatically occurs—you naturally begin to pay attention, adopt a sense of wonder, and become aware of what's happening around you.

1. When faced with information, what questions do you ask? Have they been asked before?

2. When a fact is presented to you, ask why it is a fact. Ask what objective evidence makes it a fact. Pay attention to the information.

3. Pay attention to your breathing. Focus internally. Open your senses.

4. If faced with a fact that you have judgments about, note that. Continue to focus on your breathing.

5. Ask what other explanations might make the fact valid. Consider it from several different directions.

6. If you are faced with a fact that angers you, note that. From your centered position, let the anger pass.

7. Look at the fact without emotion. Look at it from the opposite point of view from yours.

7

Intentional Reflection

Time

5 Minutes

Best for

Enhancing mindfulness

Learning from prior interactions is an important part of knowing how to communicate. Journaling—keeping a record of the moments that make your life special in small or great ways—augments your mindfulness practice. Detailing the trail of thoughts and experiences that scroll across your conscious-ness every day memorializes them and allows you to expand your experience. The aspect of journal-ing in this exercise is meant to focus on recording and remembering your interactions. Keeping a small notebook with you allows you to keep track of the interactions you have during the day, your emotional reactions to them, and how you behaved in response.

1. Monitor your interactions with others throughout the day. Pay particular attention to the feelings that emerge for you.

2. After an interchange, take a few minutes to focus on your breath and be open to your senses. If you were upset by what happened, you might find that it is more difficult to calm down. Take slow, deep breaths.

3. After opening yourself, think back to the interaction and make a journal entry of the day, the time, who you were interacting with, what you felt, and what happened.

4. As you reflect, ask yourself if you were satisfied with the result of the exchange. Ask if you felt understood. Make a note about how you felt.

5. If you were happy with the outcome, note what you did to make that happen. If you wanted a different outcome, think about what you would have wanted and what you can do the next time to make that happen.

VALUES CLARIFICATION

It is very common to spend a great deal of time or energy pursuing a career or a pastime only to find out that after all the effort, it brought no satisfaction. You might be told as a child that you should follow a certain course of study. Often, monetary success is a goal. Sometimes you might take the earnest advice of parents: "You should be a lawyer." "You should be a doctor." Values clarification is an important exercise to follow when you are communicating and want to keep track of what is important to you. In addition, it can help you maximize your satisfaction in life. It consists of looking at a list of pursuits that people find gratifying or important and developing a hierarchy of the pursuits that are important to you. If you find that you are investing yourself in efforts that really are not most important, you can change the things you do to be more in line with your values. The steps in the following two exercises are designed to help you assess your choices.

8

Clarifying What Is Important

Time

5 minutes for each activity

Best for

Finding more satisfaction in life

This section is on developing self-awareness, or the knowledge of your own values, motivations, and sense of purpose in the world. Why is that important for reducing stressful communication? Knowing who you are gives you the power to interact with others from a position of strength. One of the benefits of mindfulness is being able to reflect on yourself in an unbiased and nonjudgmental way. At times you may follow a course that is not in line with what is important to you. Clarifying your values allows you to pay attention to what is really important to you. This exercise will explore ways that you can learn more about yourself.

1. Rank these values in terms of their importance to you, with 1 being the least important and 6 the most important.

   wealth

   success

   honesty

   trust

   family

   awards and public recognition

2. Rank these values in terms of their importance to you, with 1 being the least important and 6 the most important.

   free time

   independence

   knowledge

   friends

   power

   love

3. Sit or lie down in a comfortable position in a quiet place. Focus on slow, deep breaths. Let yourself relax as you continue to stay focused on the present. Look at your rankings and determine if they match the ways you spend your time. Do your choices match the things or relationships on which you place value?

4. If you find discrepancies, make a list of what you would like to change.

5. Think of strategies that might enable you to change your priorities.

6. As you contemplate this, notice any feelings that emerge and see if you can put together a plan of action.

9

Meet
and Greet

Time

10 Minutes

Best for

Overcoming shyness

If you are shy, you know how difficult some social interactions can be, particularly with people you do not know. The sensitivity that other people will notice something about you or that you might be judged in any way might make you feel so uncomfortable in social situations that you may even avoid them. Mindfulness can be a powerful tool to combat shyness. This exercise will help you explore the thinking behind shyness and give you ways to change how you handle it.

1. Plan to go somewhere where there will be social interaction with strangers. Before entering the room, take slow, deep breaths and let yourself feel what you are aware of. What do you hear, see, smell? Being as open as you can, identify any thoughts that come across your mind.

2. Be conscious of your instinctive response. Do you want to leave? Do you want to sit somewhere out of sight? Do you want to go in and speak with people?

3. Despite what you may desire, enter the room. Again, remaining as open as you can, identify the sensations you see, hear, or feel. Identify them and just observe them. Stay in the present moment. Warning! This may be uncomfortable.

4. Stay with the feelings. Perhaps to your surprise, they should fade.

5. In order to stop feeling uncomfortable, you must do the things that make you uncomfortable.

6. A powerful technique was developed by Dr. David Burns, in his book *Intimate Connections,* called Smile and Hello. Walk up to any stranger, smile at them, and say, "Hello."

7. Go to another person you do not know. Do the same thing. Each time, stay in a focused state, monitoring your experience through mindfulness. When you are aware of any fearful feeling, be aware of it and let yourself feel it, and it will pass.

8. Continue to use Smile and Hello on the street. You will be filled with a new joy when you see how many people smile back at you.

10

Fielding the Curve Balls

Time

5 Minutes

Best for

Sidestepping hostile interactions

Every day you engage in interactions with others. Often, these are pleasant and cooperative. Sometimes, however, the person you are speaking with is in a foul mood or is irritable for some other reason. Have you ever noticed how when someone says something to you that is not nice, it is tempting to say something not nice back? This is a function of an action-reaction pattern. Every action evokes a reaction, usually of similar mood and intensity. It actually may take effort not to respond in kind. This exercise will help you stay centered and contained in hostile interactions.

1. In any interaction with another person, take a breath. Let yourself feel the ground beneath your feet. Let yourself feel open to sensations that may arise.

2. If the person you are speaking with is aggressive or hostile, you will probably have an emotional response. Pay attention to any physical cues. Do you feel your heart speed up? Do you feel flushed? Do you feel uncomfortable?

3. As you become aware of your emotions, continue to breathe. Stay focused on your breath. Be aware of any other sensations you may be experiencing.

4. The key is to maintain a distance from your emotions. Continue to focus on your breath and on the thoughts. Let yourself be an observer of the emotion from the other person, staying centered and in touch with your breathing.

5. When you start to feel the other person's emotion, stand back and let the words and feelings float past you.

6. Now you will be able to consciously and thoughtfully determine how best to handle the situation.

Chapter 6

Mindfulness on the Go

Mindfulness can help you stay calm, perform better in all aspects of your life, and reduce stress. One benefit of this process is that you can take it with you wherever you go and in whatever you do. This chapter addresses the many ways you can use mindfulness on the go. Although the process of centering yourself and staying open is the same as in previous chapters, you will learn how to apply mindfulness to everyday activities.

1

Mindfulness Morning

Time

5 minutes
each morning

Best for

Starting
your day

Starting your morning the right way can set the tone for the rest of the day. Mindfulness is a great tool for stabilizing your moods and your responses to the stress of life. During an average day, you will be bombarded by many stimuli. You will face stresses and struggles. It takes conscious effort to balance yourself in the face of all of them. You may find yourself reacting without thinking, acting on autopilot, and ending up feeling drained.

Studies have shown that the way you center yourself in the morning can build a buffer for you that makes it all easier. This exercise will show you how to get your day off to a positive start.

1. Instead of jumping out of bed immediately, give yourself a few minutes to transition from sleep to wakefulness.

2. Attend to your needs, then perform a mental check of things you must do in the morning, such as pack lunches for the kids. You should plan this exercise around those duties.

3. Find a quiet place and take slow, deep breaths. Concentrate on the present moment and let go of all the thoughts about the coming day. Do this for 5 minutes.

4. Think of one thing you are grateful for. Bask in the glow of that thought. Focus on your gratitude as you breathe.

5. As you move forward with the rest of your day, incorporate your awareness into each activity. If you shower or take a bath, do it consciously, feeling the sensations and listening to the sounds.

6. If you are making breakfast, pay attention to the sounds, smells, and textures of each task. If you are cracking an egg, listen to the shell breaking. Feel the pressure on your fingers when it cracks. Hear the sizzle when it hits the frying pan.

7. Mindfully go through the rest of the breakfast, being aware of taste and texture.

8. After the meal, hear the sound and splash of the water as you wash your plate. The goal is to stay aware and focused to clear your mind of clutter. When you accomplish this, your mind will be more effective throughout the day.

9. Getting your children ready for school can make it difficult to maintain your focused state. Before reacting to a demand or to resistance to one of your demands, identify your emotions. If you become frustrated or angry, recognize the emotion and its effect on your body. Neutralize it by taking three deep breaths. Think of what you need to make happen, and do not react.

2

Using
Social Media

Time

5 Minutes

*Best
for*

**Preventing
jealousy
and envy**

Social media has revolutionized the world. The different platforms—Facebook, Snapchat, Instagram, Twitter—have also created a number of problems. One problem is that they can make you feel bad. People usually only post pictures of times when they are happy. If you happen to be feeling bad, you may start comparing your life to your perception of theirs, and you may feel bad unnecessarily. Mindfulness is a wonderful antidote to the toxic effects of social media.

1. Before using any social media platform, sit quietly for a moment. Breathe deeply and open your senses to your experience. Do this until you feel in touch with your body and all your senses.

2. Before logging on to your Facebook page or any other social media platform, stop and ask yourself what your intention is. Do you want to catch up with friends? Do you want to see more of your feed? Notice your purpose.

3. Choose what you look at and whom you follow. If you are hurting from a failed romance, do not follow your ex-partner unless you want to feel bad. If you are looking at your friend's amazing vacation photos from Puerto Vallarta, unless you have had a vacation recently or are planning one, you may feel envious or blue. Your objective is to stay focused and centered and not distracted by thoughts that make you feel bad.

4. Take some deep breaths. Allow your senses to open and see if you can get into the present moment. If you can't, keep taking slow, deep breaths until you do.

5. When you see posts that make you feel bad, such as a friend's vacation pictures, pay close attention to your body's reactions. Do you feel tense? Warm? Chills? Note any physical sensation.

6. Now pay attention to any feelings you have, whether happy, sad, mad, scared, or jealous. If you do become aware of emotions, just notice them. As with noticing your sensations of sound, sight, and touch, notice that you are having a thought, e.g., *I am having a thought of envy* rather than *I am envious*.

7. Stay focused and let the envy float by. Do not get attached to it. Continue to breathe deeply.

8. Notice any other feelings that come up as you proceed. If they are negative feelings, see them as a response to thoughts and let the thoughts float past you.

3

Beating the Commuter Blues

Time

**The length of
your commute**

*Best
for*

**Traveling to
and from work**

Fifty-four percent of Americans commute to work.
Studies have shown that getting to the train on time,
dealing with crowded cars, and putting up with other
passengers who may be unpleasant all create stress.
If you drive to work, traffic jams and rude drivers
also put you under stress. There is not much you
can do about changing the stressful conditions of a
daily commute, but you do have control over your
response to them. Mindfulness is a very effective way
to balance your mood during what may be one of the
most stressful activities of the day.

1. Practice this mindfulness exercise before leaving for your commute. Carrying a peaceful state of mind into a commute can make it easier.

2. The key to a less stressful commute is to stop the thoughts that get you upset. Think about one of your more stressful commutes and identify the most difficult parts. What are the thoughts that create the stress? *This is so uncomfortable. I can't stand crowds. I don't like being delayed.* These thoughts are stressful due to the frustration (anger) you feel from being unable to do anything about the conditions.

3. If you find unpleasant emotions controlling how you feel, take slow, deep breaths. Focus on your senses. Let yourself stay perfectly in the present moment. If you experience an angry thought, identify it and say, *I am having an angry thought* rather than *I am angry.*

4. If you are commuting on public transportation, you might also use a meditation app that offers a guided meditation the same length as your commute. Alternatively, you can put on music that you enjoy to block out the unpleasantness and help pass the time.

5. If you commute by car, mindfulness is a perfect way to pass the time. Rather than thinking about all you have to do that day or all you did not do the day before, focus perfectly on the present moment. Take a deep breath, letting your stomach expand. Focus on the sensation of sitting while you drive. Listen to the sounds that you hear. Look at the colors and shapes of the buildings or fields that you pass. By staying perfectly in the present, you will avoid getting caught up in your own emotions.

6. If you are in your car and become frustrated, stay focused on your physical experience. If you get angry, try to see the anger as a thought and let it go. You will find that it is not the commute that creates the stress. It is how you look at it.

4

Working It Out

Time

30 to 60 Minutes

Best for

Exercising

The gym is an important place for many people. Some people use it because it feels good. Others exercise because it keeps them healthy. Still others use the gym to release stress. How do you use your gym time? Do you rush through your workout to finish it as soon as you can, or do you savor it? Adding mindfulness can add depth to the experience, which allows you to enjoy it in a different way.

1. Before starting the exercise, take some deep breaths to center yourself.

2. Open your senses. Focus on everything you hear, see, or touch, one input at a time.

3. Focus on your breathing.

4. If you are using the treadmill, start slowly. Concentrate on your breathing. As you walk or run faster, concentrate on the sensation of your feet landing on the treadmill. Focus on your breath. Feel the movement of your arms or the pressure of your hands on the handrails.

5. Focus on your breath again. As you increase your pace, focus on the extra pressure on your quadricep and calf muscles. Focus on the pressure in your lungs.

6. As you slow down, focus on how your body feels. Are you energized? Tired? Exhilarated?

7. If lifting weights, start by taking a deep breath. Even if you are used to a workout routine with weights, start very slowly.

8. Be aware of each sensation. If you are using free weights, balance yourself. Feel the tension increase in your muscles as you lift.

9. Focus on your breathing. Feel the breath come into your lungs as you lift.

10. Start slowly, concentrating on the tension on your muscles. As you increase the pressure, notice the difference in how it feels against your muscles. Try to focus as specifically as you can on each part of your muscle.

11. As you get to the end of your routine, take time to cool off.

12. Drink water. Feel the coolness of the water against the inside of your mouth and throat.

13. Sit down and feel your heart beat. Take another breath.

14. Think about what you were grateful for in this workout.

5

Peaceful Shopping

Time

5 to 60 Minutes

Best for

Shopping at stores

I am guessing you spent more time visiting stores 10 years ago than you do now. With everything from clothing to groceries available online, there are fewer and fewer reasons to go to a store. Too often shopping is a race against time: You need to get home to make dinner or you have to get back to your office. It is rare to savor the moments. Other times it can be annoying to not find the item you are looking for, or every size but yours is available. If you are in a department store, you may not even know which department to go to. If you do still shop the old-fashioned way, or you would like a less stressful experience, perform this mindfulness exercise.

1. The nature of the experience should be the same no matter where you shop.

2. Beforehand, prepare a list of everything you need. As you enter the store, take a long, deep breath. Center yourself and open your senses.

3. Walk slowly through the store. Pay attention to each stimulus as you become aware of it. What colors do you see? What smells are in the air? What sounds do you hear? Listen as they overlap.

4. As you walk through the aisles, notice what thoughts arise. Try to see them as just thoughts and focus again on the physical experience.

5. Walk through the different sections. If you are in a grocery store, pick up a fruit and feel its weight and texture. Smell it.

6. Move on, feeling your body as you walk. Look at the people around you. What do they look like? As you look around, what are you attracted to? Identify any emotion, however slight.

7. If you are in a clothing store, pay attention to your reaction to the colors, the textures. Walk around, feeling your body as you move.

8. Feel the tension in your arm as you take something off a rack. Note your decision of whether to buy a certain item. What is your process of calculation?

9. Observe yourself internally, your thinking and feeling, and your ultimate action.

6

Ho, Ho, Holidays

Time

5 Minutes

Best for

Holiday events

The holidays are a complex time with much to do. Preparations, buying presents, and attending parties take time and can put pressure on you. Families come together during the holidays, and family interactions are rarely simple; there is closeness and sometimes there is tension. Alternatively, one may not have family, and the holidays are hard because of that. All of this is under the guise of a holiday that should be joyous. Mindfulness is a wonderful tool to keep you in a positive frame of mind.

1. The key to not feeling bad at holiday time is to pay attention to what you are feeling. If you are harried or feel under pressure, recognize it. If you are excited and happy, or sad and lonely, identify it.

2. When you do have a feeling, take a breath and focus on being centered and the sensations in your body. Become aware of your surroundings. Open yourself to your senses, and concentrate on your breath. How you feel is based on what you are thinking. If you see thoughts interfering with that state, notice that you are having a thought. Do not get into the content of it, and let it pass by. Use deep breaths to stay focused on your body and to stay away from the painful thoughts.

3. If you are having a family holiday celebration, first consider your objective. Do you want to change their minds about an issue? Do you want to have a warm and pleasant time? Do you want to make a point about something that happened in the past? You can make any of these things happen. When you interact with family members, be aware of any emotions that arise. Pay attention to the physical cues of them. Tension comes from thoughts that make you tense. If you have such a thought, recognize that you are having a thought, and focus on your internal state.

4. Mindfully listen to what the other person is saying.

5. Respond by showing understanding, and if that causes you to have a feeling, take a deep breath, focus on your sensations, and notice that you are having the thought and the feeling. Stay internally focused.

7

Everyday People

Time

5 Minutes

Best for

Calming down during difficult interactions

Some people interact with others as though they have a chip on their shoulder. They might be aggressive, unreasonable, insensitive, or provocative. Being in their presence creates stress. They are difficult to deal with. If someone acts in a difficult manner around you, you might feel angry or hurt or upset. Those emotions make you react. Being mindful allows you to avoid reacting by detaching from those emotions. Once your emotions do not control your behavior, you will have more options for handling difficult people.

1. When you encounter someone who acts in a difficult way around you, you will have certain feelings. The first step is to observe that you are having such a reaction. Notice your physical cues. Identify the emotions. Take a deep breath. Distance yourself from the situation by focusing on your breath and your senses. Stay focused and centered.

2. Without acting, assess the situation. What does the person want from you, or what are they trying to say?

3. While listening mindfully and not reacting, consider your options for responding.

4. Put yourself in their shoes and see if you can understand how they feel. If you can understand, share that with them. Try saying, *I hear you saying . . . and I would guess you feel . . . (annoyed, sad, frustrated).* Then ask if you are understanding correctly.

5. If the person is still acting provocatively, identify your feelings. Take another deep breath and focus on your senses. You need to assess what the best move is to accomplish your objective. Being straightforward is often effective: *I feel like you want to have an argument with me.*

6. From your peaceful place, note that you are having a feeling rather than being in it: *I am having the feeling of anger* instead of *I am angry.*

7. Determine your options to handle the person without emotions controlling your behavior.

8

Getting the Job Done

Time

5 Minutes

Best for

Household chores

How do you feel about doing chores? If something has to get done, do you get it done? The word *chore* implies that the task is mandated rather than chosen. The purpose of this exercise is, in part, to help you get chores done more easily. The other is to help you do them mindfully. Mindfulness connects you fully to the activity in which you are engaged. You become part of it.

1. Start by taking a slow, deep breath. Open yourself to your senses.

2. Let's use doing the laundry as an example. When you think of having a pile of laundry to do, what do you think of? Pay attention to your physical reaction. Do you get distracted and start looking at other things around the room? Do you dread making the effort? Pay attention to both your physical sensations and your emotions.

3. If you are distracted, notice that and bring yourself back to center. Pay attention to the part of your mind that does not want to do the laundry. Recognize that you are experiencing a thought about not wanting to do the chore.

4. Go to the laundry room or the laundromat. As you stay focused on your breathing, feel the sensations on your hands as you take the clothing out of the laundry bag. Listen to the rustle of the fabric. As you place the laundry into the washer, notice how the clothes crumple together inside the cylinder.

5. As you prepare the laundry detergent, if it is powder, focus on its texture and smell. Listen to the sound as you pour it on the clothing. If it is liquid, notice its color and fragrance.

6. When you close the door to the washing machine, listen to the sound. As you turn on the washer, feel the pressure against your fingers and wrist.

7. Pay attention to any feelings. Do you feel accomplished? Are you unhappy about having to wait for the cycle to finish, or are you excited that you can go out and return when it's done? Do you have a feeling of relief to have completed the chore? Note whether you enjoyed this chore while being mindful.

9

Give Yourself a Break

Time

5 Minutes

Best for

Enjoying time off

Downtime is defined as leisure time, such as having time off between periods of work. Our lives are very busy. You may not even experience much downtime in your life. Yet it is critically important for your body and for your brain to take a break. Stress is caused by having more to do than time in which to do it. It is also caused by the thoughts that constantly bombard you about everything you have to do. Mindfulness allows you to experience life more fully without judgments or distracting thoughts. Applying this exercise to your downtime has great rewards, such as increasing the enjoyment you feel.

1. The next time you have time off, pick one activity to do mindfully. You can probably think of a number of examples. Here, let's use the example of watching a ball game on TV. Focus on your intention. You will come up against typical thought patterns you use, even when watching a ball game.

2. Before you turn on the TV, take a deep breath and focus on your sensations in the moment.

3. When you look around the room, what do you see? Slowly look at each object and take in the colors and shapes. Now turn on the TV. Do you have any feelings, such as excitement or anticipation? If so, recognize them. Take another deep breath and let yourself focus inwardly. Observe the thought and stay centered on your experience.

4. As the TV comes on, notice the sounds. Look at the screen as it comes alive. Notice any feelings of anticipation.

5. As you watch the game, recognize your feelings of excitement, disappointment, boredom. When you do, focus again on your breath and any other sensations you have. Note any feelings, and continue to stay focused and centered. When you feel excited, let yourself feel the physical effects of it.

6. Use the same centered focus for every leisure activity—for example, going to a baseball game. As you enter the ballpark, what do you see? What do you hear? Smell? Feel?

7. Let your senses take in all that is there. Now take a deep breath and focus internally. Do you have any thoughts or feelings? Are you upset that your team lost the last game, or are you excited that your favorite player hit the record number of home runs? If so, notice it. Feel the levels of excitement and the physical cues.

8. Assuming you eat hot dogs, get one. First, get centered. What does it smell like? Take a small bite. Chew it more than you usually would. Can you taste the layers of flavor?

10

Mindful Slumber

Time

5 Minutes

Best for

Preparing for sleep

You spend over one-third of your life in your bed. It is a place of dreams and rejuvenation. You most likely see it as just your bed. You stay up until you go to bed, and you get up and do everything you do in the day, and then you go to bed. One of the beautiful attributes of mindfulness is that it allows you to savor life. So often we rush and rush and never stop to feel what we are experiencing. This segment is to help you use mindfulness to appreciate this nightly companion.

1. At night, as you get ready for bed, consciously slow down. Pay attention to any feelings you are having. Are you tired? Do you have any emotions? Open your senses. Take a deep breath. Pay attention to the things you do before bed. Very consciously brush your teeth and wash your face, feeling the warmth or coolness of the water and the texture of the towel. Do not rush.

2. What do you do in bed before going to sleep? Do you read or watch TV, or are you intimate with a partner?

3. Whichever activity, try to experience it as fully as possible. For example, if you are reading, feel the texture of the page when you turn it. If reading on a Kindle, notice the shading of the light. Pay attention as the pages flip. Take in the content.

4. When it is time to sleep, start by taking three slow, deep breaths. Focus on the sensations of lying down and having the bed support you. Feel the sensation of your muscles starting to relax. Feel the pillow under your head.

5. Let your muscles relax, and feel your body sink into the mattress. Feel each sensation as you breathe, and feel your bed supporting your sleepy self.

6. Let yourself take in the entire experience.

Resources

Websites

Center for Mindfulness in Medicine, Health Care, and Society—
University of Massachusetts
UMassMed.edu/cfm

Massachusetts General Hospital—MGH Psychiatry Academy
Online Courses
MGHCME.org/page/benson_henry_institute_for_mind_body_medicine

Mayo Clinic Mindfulness Exercises
MayoClinic.org/healthy-lifestyle/consumer-health/in-depth
/mindfulness-exercises/art-20046356

Mindfulnet
Mindfulnet.org

Mindful
Mindful.org

PsychCentral
PsychCentral.com

Sounds True
SoundsTrue.com

UCLA Mindful Awareness Research Center
UCLAHealth.org/marc

Verywell Mind
VerywellMind.com/mindfulness-exercises-for-everyday-life-3145187

YogiApproved
YogiApproved.com

Books

Baer, R. A., ed. *Mindfulness-Based Treatment Approaches: Clinician's Guide to Evidence Base and Applications*. San Diego, CA: Elsevier, 2006.

Burns, D. *Feeling Good: The New Mood Therapy*. New York, NY: William Morrow, 1980.

Burns, D. *When Panic Attacks*. New York, NY: Morgan Roads, 2006.

Burns, D. *Feeling Good Together*. New York, NY: Broadway Books, 2008.

Bushe, G. R. *The Appreciative Inquiry Model*. In *Encyclopedia of Management Theory 1*, edited by E. H. Kessler, 41–44. Thousand Oaks, CA: Sage Publications, 2013.

Cameron, Julia. *The Artist's Way*. New York, NY: Penguin Random House, 2016.

Cooperrider, D. and D. Whitney. *Appreciative Inquiry: A Positive Revolution in Change*. San Francisco: Berrett-Koehler Publishers, 2005.

Cooperrider, D. L. and S. Srivastva. "Appreciative Inquiry in Organizational Life." In Woodman, R. W. and W. A. Pasmore. *Research in Organizational Change and Development* 1 (1987): 129–169.

Covey, Stephen. *The 7 Habits of Highly Effective Families*. New York, NY: St. Martin's Press, 1997.

Crick, R. Deakin "Learning How to Learn: The Dynamic Assessment of Learning Power." *The Curriculum Journal* 18, no. 2 (2007): 135–153.

Eisler, Melissa. *Type A's Guide to Mindfulness: Meditation for Busy Minds and Busy People*. Mindful Minutes Press, 2016.

Gilles, David. *Mindful Work: How Meditation Is Changing Business from the Inside Out*. New York, NY: Eamon Dolan/Houghton Mifflin, 2015.

Hanson, Rick. *Just One Thing: Developing a Buddha Brain One Simple Practice at a Time*. Oakland, CA: New Harbinger, 2011.

Kahneman, Daniel. *Thinking Fast and Slow*. New York, NY: Farrar, Straus and Giroux, 2011.

Stavros, Jacqueline, Lindsey Godwin, David Lindsey, and David Cooperrider. "Appreciative Inquiry: Organization Development and the Strengths Revolution." In *Practicing Organization Development: A Guide to Leading Change and Transformation* (4th ed.), edited by William Rothwell, Roland Sullivan, and Jacqueline Stavros. Hoboken, NJ: Wiley, 2015.

Tartakovsky, M. "6 Mindful Ways to Minimize Holiday Stress." PsychCentral. Accessed December 25, 2012. https://psychcentral.com /blog/6-mindful-ways-to-minimize-holiday-stress

Willard, Christopher. *Growing Up Mindful*. Boulder, CO: Sounds True Press, 2016.

Winston, D., and S. Smalley. *Fully Present: The Science, Art, and Practice of Mindfulness*. Philadelphia, PA: Ingram, 2010.

Zinn, J. K. *Full Catastrophe Living: Using the Wisdom of Your Body and Mind to Face Stress, Pain, and Illness* (Revised Edition). New York, NY: Bantam Press, 2013.

Zinn, J. K. *Wherever You Go, There You Are: Mindfulness Meditation in Everyday Life*. New York, NY: Hachette, 2005.

References

Bazarko, Dawn, R. A. Cate, F. Azocar, and M. J. Kreitzer. "The Impact of an Innovative Mindfulness-Based Stress Reduction Program on the Health and Well-Being of Nurses Employed in a Corporate Setting." *J Workplace Behavioral Health* 28 no. 2 (April 2013): 107–133. https://doi.org/10.1080/15555240.2013.779518.

Cohen, Sheldon, D. Janicki-Deverts, W. J. Doyle, G. E. Miller, E. Frank, B. S. Rabin, and R. B. Turner. "Chronic Stress, Glucocorticoid Receptor Resistance, Inflammation, and Disease Risk." *PNAS* 109 no. 16 (April 2012): 5995–5999. https://doi.org/10.1073/pnas.1118355109

Domar, Alice D., K. L. Rooney, B. Wiegand, E. J. Orav, M. M. Alper, B. M. Berger, and J. Nikolovski. "Impact of a Group Mind/Body Intervention on Pregnancy Rates in IVF Patients." *Fertil Steril* 95, no. 7 (June 2011): 2269–2273. https://doi.org/10.1016/j.fertnstert.2011.03.046.

Gouin, Jean-Philippe, and J. K. Kiecolt-Glaser. "The Impact of Psychological Stress on Wound Healing: Methods and Mechanisms." *Immunology and Allergy Clinics of North America* 31, no. 1 (February 2011): 81–93. https://doi.org/10.1016/j.iac.2010.09.010.

National Sleep Foundation. "Insomnia." Accessed June 5, 2019. https://www
.sleepfoundation.org/sleep-disorders/insomnia

Nery, Simone F., S. P. C. Paiva, É. L. Vieira, A. B. Barbosa, E. M. Sant'Anna, M.
Casalechi, C. Dela Cruz, A. L. Teixeira, and F. M. Reis. "Mindfulness-Based
Program for Stress Reduction in Infertile Women: Randomized Controlled
Trial." *Stress and Health* 35 (2019): 49–58. https://doi.org/10.1002
/smi.2839.

Index

Acknowledgments

I want to thank the folks at Callisto Media who made this such an enjoyable project.

In my professional sphere, I want to acknowledge Dr. David Burns, who has informed my professional work for the past seven years. I did not learn mindfulness from him. He is a master in CBT, and he taught me an amazingly powerful way to help my patients through a form of cognitive therapy he developed called TEAM-CBT. When I first saw this approach, I couldn't believe how brilliant and effective it was. I then had the honor to study with him. His graciousness, humility, and brilliance will inspire me forever.

About the Author

 **Dr. Robert Schachter** is a psychologist and an assistant clinical professor in the Department of Psychiatry of The Icahn School of Medicine at Mount Sinai in New York, where he teaches stress management and cognitive therapy. Dr. Schachter is the director of Stress Centers of New York and has worked extensively in the area of stress management and motivation. He works with companies in industry, with individuals, and with groups.

He has lectured nationally and internationally and is an experienced talk show guest, having appeared on MSNBC, CNN, Fox Cable Network, *Inside Edition, Geraldo, Regis and Kathy Lee, CBS This Morning, Fox News, Good Day New York, Maury Povich*, and local news shows. Dr. Schachter has completed two national media tours and has been quoted as an authority in hundreds of publications including *Ladies' Home Journal, Child, Parenting, Time, New York Times, U.S. News and World Report*, and *USA Today*.

His highly acclaimed book, *When Your Child Is Afraid*, was published by Simon and Schuster in 1988. He also developed and produced *The Sleep Tape*, 1988, Simon and Schuster Video, an interactive video treatment for insomnia.

He is a founding fellow and past president of the New York City Cognitive and Behavioral Therapy Association.